A Country
Divided

1833–1868

DEBATABLE ISSUES
IN U.S. HISTORY

VOLUME THREE

A Country Divided

1833–1868

GREENWOOD PRESS
Westport, Connecticut - London

Library of Congress Cataloging-in-Publication Data

Debatable issues in U.S. history / by Creative Media Applications.
        p. cm.—(Middle school reference)
    Includes bibliographical references and index.
ISBN 0–313–32910–9 (set : alk. paper)—ISBN 0–313–32911–7 (v. 1 : alk. paper)—
ISBN 0–313–32912–5 (v. 2 : alk. paper)—ISBN 0–313–32913–3 (v. 3 : alk. paper)—
ISBN 0–313–32914–1 (v. 4 : alk. paper)—ISBN 0–313–32915–X (v. 5 : alk. paper)
    1. United States—History—Miscellanea—Juvenile literature.
2. United States—Politics and government—Miscellanea—Juvenile literature.
3. United States—Social conditions—Miscellanea—Juvenile literature.
4. Critical thinking—Study and teaching (Middle school)—United States.
[1. United States—History. 2. United States—Politics and
government.] I. Creative Media Applications. II. Series.
E178.3.D35   2004
973—dc22   2003056802

British Library Cataloguing in Publication Data is available.

Library of Congress Catalog Card Number: 2003056802
ISBN: 0–313–32910–9 (set)
            0–313–32911–7 (vol. 1)
            0–313–32912–5 (vol. 2)
            0–313–32913–3 (vol. 3)
            0–313–32914–1 (vol. 4)
            0–313–32925–X (vol. 5)

First published in 2004

Greenwood Press, 88 Post Road West, Westport, CT 06881
An imprint of Greenwood Publishing Group, Inc.
www.greenwood.com

Printed in the United States of America

∞™
The paper used in this book complies with the Permanent Paper Standard issued by the
National Information Standards Organization (Z39.48–1984).

10 9 8 7 6 5 4 3 2 1

A Creative Media Applications, Inc. Production
Writer: Michael Burgan
Design and Production: Fabia Wargin Design
Editor: Matt Levine
Copyeditor: Laurie Lieb
Proofreader: Betty Pessagno
Indexer: Nara Wood
Associated Press Photo Researcher: Yvette Reyes
Consultant: Mel Urofsky, Professor Emeritus of History at Virginia Commonwealth University

Photo credits:
© PictureHistory *pages* 5, 6, 8, 39, 49, 61, 68, 71, 74, 76, 79, 81, 83, 87, 91, 92, 94, 97, 101,
105, 108, 111, 112, 116, 121, , 127, 129, 130, 131
© Hulton Archives/Getty Images *pages* 11, 16, 26
© CORBIS *pages* 21, 23, 65
© Bettmann/CORBIS *pages* 19, 31, 33, 41, 45, 51, 55, 56

Contents

Open debate among its citizens is one of the most important characteristics of a democratic nation like the United States. Newspapers and other media have always been important contributors to these debates. The ability of citizens to express their ideas freely helps their leaders know what issues are important to them.

Introduction

*W*hen people come together in a community, they face important decisions about how to run their affairs. Since everyone does not think alike, have the same feelings, or share the same interests, disagreements often arise over key issues.

In a democratic society such as the United States, public debate helps leaders decide what action to take on the most important issues. The debates might start in Congress or another branch of the government. They are often carried on in the media, and they continue in homes, in offices, and wherever concerned citizens gather.

The five volumes of *Debatable Issues in U.S. History* look at some of the most important issues that have sparked political and social debates, from colonial times to the present day. Some of the issues have been local, such as the dispute between Roger Williams and the Puritan leaders of Massachusetts. Williams struggled to introduce the idea of religious freedom in a community that wanted just one kind of religious worship. Other issues—segregation, for example—had special significance for a large group of people. African Americans, who had once been forced to live in slavery, had to endure lingering prejudice even when they received their freedom during and after the Civil War (1861–1865). Some of the most important issues have touched all Americans, as the country's leaders considered whether to go to war in times of international crisis. The 2003 war in Iraq is just the latest example of that debate.

Throughout American history, certain types of issues have appeared over and over. The details may change, but Americans continue to argue over such things as: How much power should

> How much power should the national government have?

the national government have? How does society balance personal freedom with the need to protect the common good? Which political party has the best vision for strengthening the country? Who should America choose as its friends and its enemies around the world?

> How does society balance personal freedom with the need to protect the common good?

Historians have debated the importance of certain events for hundreds of years. New facts emerge, or interpretations change as the world changes. From the historians' view, almost any issue is debatable. This series, however, focuses on the events and issues that Americans debated as they occurred. Today, few people would question whether the American colonies should have declared their independence from Great Britain; it seems almost impossible to imagine anything else happening. However, to the Americans of the day, the issue was not so clear-cut. Colonial leaders strongly disagreed on what action to take in the months before Thomas Jefferson wrote the Declaration of Independence.

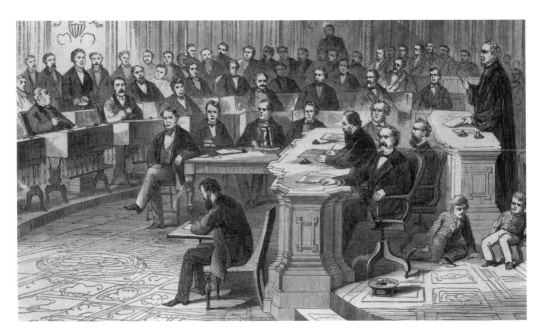

Debate over important issues has always been a vital component of life in the United States. In fact, the country's very formation took place amid intense debate over radical new ideas about government. The impeachment trial of President Andrew Johnson in 1868, pictured above, showed that the debate would continue.

At times in the past, debate over key issues might have been limited. From the seventeenth century through most of the nineteenth century, transportation and communication were primitive compared with today. Still, through letters, sermons, newspapers, and government documents, opposing ideas were shared and debated. The lack of electronic communication did not weaken the passion with which people held their beliefs and their desire to shape public issues.

Today, the Internet and other forms of digital communication let millions of people debate crucial issues that face the United States. Better technology, however, does not make it easier for people to settle these issues. As *Debatable Issues in U.S. History* shows, strong emotions often fuel the discussions over the issues. At times, those emotions spill out in violence. On issues that matter most, people are often unwilling to give in, modify their views, or admit that they are wrong. Those attitudes can lead to debates that last for generations. Abortion was a heated issue in 1973, when the U.S. Supreme Court ruled that a woman could legally have an abortion if she chose. Abortion remains a divisive issue today, and there is not much chance that the debate will end.

Who should America choose as its friends and its enemies around the world?

Debates and disagreements can make it hard for governments to function smoothly. Still, debate allows Americans to explore all sides of an issue. Debate can also lead to new and better ideas that no one had considered before. U.S. Supreme Court Justice William Brennan once noted that Americans have "a profound national commitment to the principle that debate on public issues should be uninhibited, robust, and wide open." That commitment first took shape in colonial America, and it continues today.

A Note to the Reader

The quotations in Debatable Issues in U.S. History *are taken from primary sources, the writings and speeches of the people debating the important issues of their time. Some of the words, phrases, and images in these sources may be offensive by today's standards, but they are an authentic example of our past history. Also, some of the quotes have been slightly changed to reflect the modern spelling of the original words or to make the meaning of the quotes clearer. All metric conversions in this book are approximate.*

CHAPTER ONE

Indian Removal

WHAT
The U.S. government moves Native American tribes from their homelands to territory west of the Mississippi River.

ISSUE
The legality and desirability of removal

WHERE
The Southeastern states

WHEN
1830s

*E*arly U.S. leaders had different opinions on how to live with the Native American tribes of the Southeast. President George Washington thought that the government could teach some of the tribes how to live and work as Europeans and white Americans did. Among the Cherokee, the U.S. government promoted farming and education, and missionaries came to teach them Christianity. The Cherokee eventually developed their own written alphabet and created a government based on the U.S. Constitution.

Other presidents, however, thought that the best way to deal with the Cherokee and neighboring tribes was to relocate them. Thomas Jefferson first considered this idea in 1803, when the United States bought the Louisiana Territory from France. The government would buy Native American lands in the Southeast and then give them new land west of the Mississippi River. The river would separate white and Native American cultures, and American settlers could move into the tribes' former lands. A small example of this "Indian removal" policy took place in 1817, under President James Monroe. The U.S. government bought some land from the Cherokee and gave them new land in Arkansas. Moving to this new land was voluntary; over the next two decades, only a few thousand Cherokee left their traditional tribal lands.

By the 1820s, Georgia was demanding that the U.S. government remove all the Cherokee within its borders. In 1802, the state had agreed to give the government some of its western lands. In exchange, U.S. leaders were supposed to sign treaties with the Cherokee, who would turn over their lands to Georgia. The Cherokee were then supposed to leave the state. The government, however, had not followed through on this deal.

Georgia's desire to force out the Cherokee grew after July 1828, when gold was discovered on their land. White miners and settlers flocked to the region, and Georgia's political leaders increased their calls for wide-scale Indian removal. They also made life difficult for the Cherokee, hoping to drive them out of Georgia.

The state passed laws that prevented the Cherokee from mining gold and took away many of their legal rights. One law prevented white missionaries from entering Cherokee lands without state permission. Georgia's leaders did not want the missionaries to help the Cherokee resist efforts to force them out of the state.

THE CHEROKEE CASES

Georgia's legal efforts against the Cherokee led to two famous U.S. Supreme Court decisions. In 1831, the tribe argued that Georgia did not have a legal right to limit the tribe's political system, since the Cherokee were an independent, foreign nation. Previous treaties with different Native American tribes had stated that the tribes were indeed independent. The Supreme Court ruled that the tribes had a special relationship with the U.S. government, but that they were not a foreign nation. The court said that it did not have the power to decide the issue between Georgia and the Cherokee. The next year, the court did agree with the tribe that Georgia did not have the right to force whites to get state permission to enter Native American lands. Georgia, however, refused to obey the court and end the policy, and President Jackson lacked the legal power to force Georgia to obey the court.

The Indian Removal Act

Shortly after the discovery of gold in Georgia, Andrew Jackson won the U.S. presidency. As a general in the U.S. Army, Jackson had fought the Creeks during the War of 1812 (1812–1815). Later, he fought the Creeks and Seminoles as he tried to take Florida from Spain. Jackson won a reputation as a great "Indian fighter." On a personal level, however, he had good relations with many Native Americans. Still, he shared a view common among whites of the era that the tribes, even those considered "civilized," were still "savages." Jackson also knew that American settlers wanted to continue moving westward into Native American lands, so new conflicts would arise.

Jackson called for an official policy of Indian removal, and in 1830, Congress passed the Indian Removal Act. The law gave Jackson the power to sign treaties with tribes who were willing to sell their lands in the Southeast and move to the "Indian Territory" west of the Mississippi River. The first treaty was signed in September, with the Choctaw, who gave up tribal lands in Alabama and Mississippi.

The Creeks signed a treaty two years later, though this was not a formal removal treaty. Instead, the Creeks agreed to give up some of their land in Alabama in return for government protection. The government also promised that the remaining Creek land would be controlled by leaders of the tribes. Over the next few years, however, white settlers clashed with the Creeks, and the government used the battles as an excuse to force the Native Americans off their homeland. Hundreds of Creeks were put in chains and marched to the Indian Territory.

Difficult Removals

The Cherokee and the Seminoles proved the hardest to move off their homelands. In 1835, Major Ridge, a Cherokee tribal leader, signed a removal treaty with the U.S. government. By this time, Georgia had taken over most of the Cherokee land and sold it to white settlers. Ridge led a faction of the tribe that moved voluntarily to the Indian Territory.

Another Cherokee leader, John Ross, represented a much larger group that resisted the removal. Ross traveled to Washington, D.C., several times, arguing that Ridge did not represent the entire tribe when he signed the removal treaty. On one trip, Ross brought a petition signed by 15,000 people who opposed removal. Congress, however, accepted the treaty as valid. In 1838, the U.S. Army and state militia troops forced Ross and his followers to obey the treaty and leave Georgia. A few hundred Cherokee managed to escape into the mountains, but the rest began a forced march along a route known today as "the Trail of Tears." Along the way, the Cherokee faced bad weather and harsh living conditions. During winter storms, noted one soldier, the people "had to sleep in the wagons and on the ground without fire." Thousands of Cherokee died during the trip. By March 1839, the last of the surviving Cherokee reached Oklahoma.

> *Fast Fact*
> Major Ridge had fought for the Americans and Andrew Jackson during the War of 1812, in battles against the Creeks.

Unlike Ross and the Cherokee, the Seminoles did not use the legal system to resist removal. They chose to fight. Although they were forced to sign a treaty in 1832, the Seminoles ignored the order to move west. Starting in 1835, they began a war that lasted seven years. Operating out of Florida's swamps, small groups of Seminoles carried out raids against American troops. The government managed to capture and remove several thousand Seminoles, losing about 1,500 soldiers in the process. A smaller number of Seminoles also died during the fighting. In 1842, U.S. leaders finally gave up on their efforts to remove the Seminoles.

Famous Figures

JOHN ROSS
(1790–1866)

John Ross was a mixed-blood Cherokee who was elected chief of the tribe in 1828. Ross had eagerly adapted to American ways. Educated by white missionaries, he spoke little Cherokee and dressed like a typical Southern gentleman. Yet he was proud of his Cherokee background, and as chief, he resisted the government's efforts to drive the Cherokee from their land. Once the Cherokee settled in Oklahoma, Ross helped his people rebuild the lifestyle that they had enjoyed in Georgia.

REMOVAL IN THE OLD NORTHWEST

Indian removal also went on in the Northwest, an area that includes present-day Ohio, Illinois, Indiana, Michigan, and Wisconsin. In 1832, several tribes that had moved westward to Iowa returned to their old lands in Illinois. They found white settlers on the land. Led by Black Hawk, a Sac native chief, the tribes tried to reclaim their rights to the land. American troops came to drive them out. In Black Hawk's War (1832), the two sides fought several small battles, in one of which American troops massacred Native American women and children. Black Hawk's defeat marked the last organized effort by the Northwestern tribes to resist removal.

The Support for Indian Removal

Americans put forth a number of arguments in favor of Indian removal. In part, removal reflected racist attitudes that some white settlers had shown since the seventeenth century. They believed that Native Americans were not civilized and that they prevented the Americans from developing land for farms and towns. One Georgia lawmaker called the Native Americans "useless" and a burden on the government. He described them as "a race not admitted to be equal to the rest of the community."

Although President Jackson held some of the common prejudices against Native Americans, he considered them a "much-injured" people. He tried to suggest that removal would benefit the tribes. If they remained in the Southeastern states, they would have to follow the laws of those states. As Georgia had shown, some state governments limited the tribes' freedom in order to acquire their land. In the Indian Territory, Jackson said, the Native Americans could live under "governments of their own choice." They would also be protected by the national government, unlike in the states. The president called removal "hard and cruel," but he thought that it was the only way Native Americans could preserve their culture. Jackson also pledged that the removals would be voluntary, though future events proved that the government did not keep its word on this matter.

Some Native Americans also saw reasons to go along with the removal, even if reluctantly. Many realized that they could not stop the movement of settlers into their lands and that they lacked the military strength to fight the Americans. When Major Ridge and his Cherokee followers decided to move, they

Fast Fact
The forced removal of the Cherokee was carried out under President Martin Van Buren, who had been elected president in 1836. Van Buren, a close associate of Andrew Jackson, shared his beliefs on Indian removal.

Fast Fact
Despite the promises made in the removal treaties, the tribes that volunteered to go west were often treated badly. The food that they received was sometimes rotten, and the medical care was poor.

believed that they were guaranteeing their tribe's survival. One leader said, "We can die, but the great Cherokee nation will be saved." The treaties also seemed to offer the tribes generous terms. The government promised to move them to their new homes and pay for food and other supplies. One treaty promised that the U.S. officials in charge of the move would be "kind and brotherly to them."

In Their Own Words

Here is part of Andrew Jackson's message to Congress in 1829, when he first called for Indian removal.

This [removal] should be voluntary, for it would be as cruel, as unjust to compel the [tribes] to abandon the graves of their fathers and seek a home in a distant land. But they should be distinctly informed that if they remain within the limits of the states they must be subject to their laws.

Indian Removal Under Attack

When President Jackson first proposed Indian removal, he met strong resistance in Congress. Some lawmakers genuinely wanted to protect the rights of the Native Americans. Others believed that Jackson should have consulted with Congress first before proposing removal. His political enemies, members of the National Republican Party, encouraged the Cherokee to take legal action in Georgia. Other opponents of the removal included church groups that tried to convert Native Americans to Christianity. These groups believed that tribal members could be taught American culture and should be allowed to live on their own lands.

Senator Theodore Frelinghuysen of New Jersey made an impassioned speech on the Indian Removal Act. He accused the government of acting illegally in its greedy effort to take Native American land.

In Congress, Senator Theodore Frelinghuysen led the attack on the Indian Removal Act. In April 1830, over the course of three days, the New Jersey lawmaker spoke for six hours against the plan. He accused the government of acting illegally in the past by breaking treaties made with the tribes. Frelinghuysen also attacked the greed that fueled the effort to take Native American land: "We have crowded the tribes upon a few miserable acres of our Southern frontier; it is all that is left to them of their once boundless forests: and still [America] cries, give! give! give!"

Other lawmakers focused on the cost of removal and the land that the Native Americans were going to receive in the West. The Indian Removal Act called for spending only $500,000. Some representatives feared that it would actually cost millions of dollars to buy tribal lands and move the Native Americans to their new homes. These criticisms later proved right, as the United States spent about $68 million on Indian removal during Jackson's presidency.

Some representatives also questioned the administration's claim that the tribes would receive good land west of the Mississippi. One representative cited a report that called the land "almost wholly unfit for [farming]," not suitable for "a people depending upon agriculture"— as the Cherokee and other tribes did.

Once the Indian Removal Act was passed, the tribes themselves began to criticize and resist removal. They argued that they had lived on the land since long before the Europeans came to North America, and they had a right to stay on it. For the Cherokee, John Ross said that the treaty that forced them off their lands was illegal. He wrote of the treaty, "We are stripped of every attribute of freedom and...legal self-defence." However, neither the tribes nor their supporters' arguments could prevent the removals.

In Their Own Words

Here is part of a speech by John Ross, outlining the treatment of the Native Americans in America.

Ever since [the whites came] we have been treated like dogs...our country and the graves of our Fathers torn from us.... The existence of the Indian nations as distinct independent communities within the limits of the United States seems to be drawing to a close.

CHAPTER TWO

The Bank War

FOUNDED A.D. MDCCXCV.

WHAT
Andrew Jackson destroys the Second Bank of the United States.

ISSUES
The usefulness of a national bank;
the president's power to veto laws

WHERE
Nationwide

WHEN
1832–1833

*D*uring Andrew Jackson's first term as president, he made the Bank of the United States (BUS) a key issue. Jackson believed that the BUS was "dangerous to liberty." He thought that the bank had too much financial power and favored the interests of the wealthy. In general, Jackson wanted the states and the people to have as much freedom and power as possible. The BUS, he thought, was an example of the national government's control over the people, so Jackson wanted to get rid of the bank.

Congress had chartered the BUS, or given it permission to form, in 1816. It was based in Philadelphia, Pennsylvania, and had offices in other cities. The bank was partly owned by the U.S. government, but most of it was owned by private investors. The BUS served as the national government's bank, holding the money that the country received from taxes. It made loans to businesses and influenced the policies of state banks. The BUS also issued bank notes, which were used like today's paper money to buy goods or pay off debts.

During 1819, the BUS was criticized for its policies. That year, the U.S. economy began to weaken, and the bank began to demand repayment of some of the loans that it had made during better times. It also made state banks pay out specie—gold or silver coins—instead of bank notes. Many banks did not have enough specie and were forced to close. The bank's policies forced many people to sell their property to pay off debts and led to about 500,000 people losing their jobs. Many people blamed the BUS for creating a financial crisis.

Although the BUS later helped the U.S. economy grow, Jackson remembered the damage that it had done in 1819. That memory, and his distrust of banks in general, partially explained his "war" on the

Fast Fact

The economic problems in 1819 were called a panic. Today, economists refer to severe downturns in the economy as recessions. Very long and deep recessions are called depressions, such as the Great Depression of the 1930s.

BUS in 1832. He also believed that the chartering of the bank had been illegal from the beginning, since the Constitution did not give Congress the power to create a national bank.

THE FIRST BUS

The BUS chartered in 1816 was the country's second national bank. The first had been chartered in 1791. Alexander Hamilton, the first U.S. secretary of the treasury, had argued that the United States needed a national bank to help pay off debts and promote investments. From the beginning, some Americans opposed the idea of a national bank, fearing the power that it would have over the states' economic interests. The first BUS closed in 1811, when its twenty-year charter ran out, and Congress chose not to renew it. Economic troubles during the War of 1812 (1812–1815) convinced Congress to charter the second BUS.

First Shots of the "War"

In December 1829, in his presidential message to Congress, Jackson only briefly mentioned the BUS. Still, he made it clear that he did not think the bank was helpful or legal. For the next three years, the bank was a major political issue. In 1836, the bank's charter was going to expire. Congress could then issue a new charter and either keep the old rules of operation or make changes. It could also kill the bank altogether by refusing to grant a charter. Many members of Jackson's party, the Democrats (formerly the Democratic-Republicans), wanted to end the bank, but it still had influential friends. Nicholas Biddle, who had been named as the bank's president in 1823, was close to several important members of Congress, such as Daniel Webster and Henry Clay. Many wealthy merchants along the East Coast also supported the BUS.

Congress seemed willing to ignore Jackson's concerns about the bank until 1836. In the Senate, however, Thomas Hart Benton of Missouri launched an attack on the BUS. During an 1831 speech, he said that the charter should not be renewed. Benton said that the bank "tends...to make the rich richer and the poor poorer."

The next year, Henry Clay, a leading National Republican, suggested that Congress should not wait until 1836 to consider the bank's charter. Clay was going to run against Jackson in the upcoming presidential election. He was confident that Jackson would not veto the charter during the race. Clay thought that Jackson would not risk losing the votes of Americans who supported the bank. If the president did veto the charter, Clay could hold that against him during the campaign. Clay also believed that if Jackson won reelection, he would certainly veto the charter later on.

During the summer of 1832, Congress granted the BUS a new charter. Clay had misjudged Jackson, because he immediately vetoed the charter. Clay had also misread how people would respond to the veto. Most favored Jackson and his attempt to limit the power of the national government. Clay made the BUS veto a major issue in the presidential race, and he lost badly.

The Final Blows

With Jackson's reelection, the supporters of the BUS knew that its future was uncertain. The president wanted to kill it right away. In 1833, Jackson announced that he was taking all the government's money out of the bank. The money would go into state banks—preferably ones run by loyal Democrats. Without the government money, the bank would lose economic power. With less power over the economy, it would also lose influence with lawmakers who might try to seek a new charter in 1836. Keeping the bank going after 1836, Jackson claimed, would be "inconsistent with the...happiness and liberties of the people."

William Duane, Jackson's secretary of the treasury, opposed removing the government's money from the BUS. He thought that only Congress had the power to make that decision. Jackson fired Duane and went ahead with his plan. Over the next year, he ended more of the bank's duties. When the country slipped into another economic panic, some lawmakers called on Jackson to return the government funds to the bank. He said that as long as he was president, the money would not return and the bank would never get another charter.

When the BUS charter expired, Biddle tried to keep the bank running as a state bank in Pennsylvania. He resigned as its president in 1839. Two years later, the bank closed for good, and investors sued Biddle for illegal dealings that he had made. After Jackson's defeat of the BUS, the United States did not have another national banking system until 1913.

Fast Fact

Before Jackson, no U.S. president had ever fired a member of his cabinet. In the past, when a president and a secretary disagreed over a policy, the cabinet member resigned.

Draw'd off from Natur 'by Zek: Downing, Neffu to Major Jack Downing.

THE DOWNFALL OF MOTHER BANK.

Printed & Publ ᵈ by H.R.Robinson, 52 Courtlandt St ᵗ N. York.

The Democrats Attack the BUS

Jackson distrusted the power of any bank and especially a powerful one like the BUS. He believed that banks were owned by the wealthy to help other wealthy people and that their policies hurt farmers and workers. Jackson also opposed the use of paper money, such as BUS bank notes. He believed in "hard" currency—gold or silver specie. Many Democrats shared Jackson's beliefs, and they welcomed the "Bank War." They remembered how people had suffered during the Panic of 1819, which was blamed on the BUS.

Jackson had real reasons to distrust the BUS. An earlier bank president had violated the bank's charter and illegally profited on its activities. Jackson was convinced that corrupt practices continued under Biddle, who, along with other bank officials, approved loans to politicians and newspaper editors to win their backing. The bank also helped defeat political candidates who opposed it.

The BUS, Jackson and others believed, had too much influence on both politics and the economy. Although it was the nation's bank, the BUS was not under direct government control. Its main focus was to make money for its investors—not necessarily to do what was best for the country. Its directors, some claimed, had too much power and did not reflect the interests of the entire country. One opponent wrote in 1834, "Its sympathies, its prejudices, are all on the side of wealth." Most of the directors were picked by the private investors who owned the bank. By 1832, a growing number of the investors were citizens of other countries. Jackson and others worried that "foreign hands" would have too much control of the bank.

In Their Own Words

Here is part of Andrew Jackson's message to Congress explaining his veto of the BUS.

When the laws undertake to…make the rich richer and the potent more powerful, the humble members of society…have a right to complain of injustice to their government…. If [government] would confine itself to equal protection…and shower its favors alike on the…rich and poor, it would be an unqualified blessing. In the act before me there seems to be a wide and unnecessary departure from these just principles.

Support for the BUS

Jackson's opponents had varying reasons for supporting the BUS. Some agreed with an 1830 report by a committee from the House of Representatives, which outlined the many positive results that the bank had on the U.S. economy. The report pointed out that the BUS had strengthened the currency, or system of money, used in the United States. The value of currency, in the form of BUS bank notes, did not change throughout the country. The BUS also made sure that the state banks backed their notes with specie, meaning that they had real value. If people did not have faith that the paper notes could be turned in for specie, they would not use it. The report concluded that "[destroying] the existing bank...after it has rendered such [useful] services to the country...would be an act rather of cruelty...than of justice."

Some lawmakers also had more selfish reasons for supporting the bank. They received special fees from Biddle, called retainers, and they had their own accounts with the bank. They also counted on the votes and financial support of merchants who wanted the bank to survive. For these members of Congress, the BUS helped support their political careers.

As the Bank War went on, Jackson stressed his belief that the BUS was unconstitutional. The bank's supporters noted that the U.S. Supreme Court had ruled that the bank was constitutional. What was unconstitutional, they argued, was Jackson's veto of the 1832 recharter. In the past, presidents had vetoed a law only if it was unconstitutional. In this case, Jackson knew that the bank was allowed under the Constitution, but he chose to ignore the Supreme Court's ruling and the will of Congress. Speaking in the Senate in 1832, Daniel Webster criticized Jackson's veto. "There was never a moment," he said, "in which any president would have been tolerated in asserting such a claim to despotic powers."

Some politicians and newspapers criticized Jackson's veto for another reason. He and other Democrats claimed that the bank's policies hurt the country's farmers and average workers. The bank's supporters called this idea unfair, and some suggested that Jackson was merely trying to stir up the "common people" and win their votes while ignoring what was good for the country. One newspaper in Maine compared the president to historical figures of the past who tried to win the support of violent mobs and rule as dictators. "All have obtained unlimited and despotic power by pretending to be the sole friend of the people and often by denouncing the rich."

The anger over Jackson's veto lasted for several years. Some lawmakers felt that Jackson was unfairly trying to claim the power to make laws. If a president could veto a law for any reason, Congress would only pass laws that it thought the president would accept. If Jackson used the veto often, he would have more influence on the lawmaking process than the Constitution meant to give presidents.

In 1834, the Senate showed its feelings toward Jackson when it censured him. A censure is a formal criticism of a political figure. The censure came after Jackson had removed government funds from the BUS. The Senate's resolution said that Jackson had "assumed upon himself authority and power not conferred by the Constitution and laws." The Senate's action marked the first censure ever of a U.S. president and showed the strong feelings that Jackson had stirred with his Bank War. Still, Jackson's decision to kill the bank was popular with most Americans. Now, future presidents would claim the same power that Jackson had, to veto laws that they did not like.

Fast Fact

The Senate voted to censure President Andrew Jackson in 1834. The censure was because Jackson had abused his authority. Jackson had transferred money from the national bank to state institutions, interfering with the bank's finances. In early 1837, the censure was stripped from the Senate records. This was largely due to the actions of Senator Thomas Hart Benton.

In Their Own Words

Here is part of Daniel Webster's speech criticizing Jackson's veto of the BUS charter.

[The veto] extends the grasp of [the] executive...over every power of the government.... It...seeks to inflame the poor against the rich; it...attacks whole classes of people, for the purpose of turning against them the prejudices...of other classes.

Famous Figures

DANIEL WEBSTER
(1782–1852)

For more than twenty years, Daniel Webster was one of the most influential members of Congress. He spent most of that time in the Senate, where he was known as a powerful speaker. Born in New Hampshire, Webster was a talented lawyer before entering politics. He argued more than 170 cases in front of the Supreme Court. Webster usually supported laws that helped New England merchants and factory owners. Twice, he served as secretary of state. In 1851, he backed the first voyage of U.S. ships to Japan.

CHAPTER THREE

The Annexation of Texas

WHAT

The United States annexes the Republic of Texas.

ISSUES

The benefit of adding Texas to the Union; the expansion of slavery

WHERE

Nationwide

WHEN

1843–1845

*I*n the early 1800s, after the United States purchased Louisiana from France, some Americans hoped to acquire Texas, too. Until just a few weeks before the United States took control of Louisiana, Spain had owned that territory and neighboring Mexico, which included Texas. The Spanish gave Louisiana to France, which then sold it to the United States. The borders of Louisiana, however, were not clearly defined, and some Americans claimed that the purchase included Texas. Spain denied this, and in 1819, the U.S. government finally agreed that it did not have a legal claim to Texas. That agreement, however, did not stop Americans from settling in Texas—and from thinking that, one day, the region would be part of the United States.

In 1810, Mexico began a war for independence from Spain. The Mexicans won their freedom in 1821. The same year, pioneer Stephen Austin led the first large settlement of Americans into Texas. Hundreds more families soon followed, creating a thriving American community in Texas.

At first, Mexico welcomed the Americans, but in 1830, the Mexican government started limiting immigration into Texas. It feared that the Americans would dominate the region. The Mexicans also began collecting a new tax that the Texans had not had to pay before. Over the next several years, the Texans clashed with the Mexican government, which was led by General Antonio López de Santa Anna. In 1835, Austin realized that he and the Texans would have to "defend our rights, our country, and ourselves by force of arms."

The Texans originally fought to end Santa Anna's rule as a dictator and restore their old freedoms. Then in March 1836, the Texans declared their independence. They lost a major battle at the Alamo, in San Antonio, but in April 1836, troops led by Sam Houston defeated Santa Anna's forces at San Jacinto. With that victory, the Texans won their independence and formed a new country—the Republic of Texas.

*After his defeat at San Jacinto in April 1836, Mexican general Santa Anna
(at right, bowing) is brought before the injured Sam Houston, commander of the
Texan forces. Now independent from Mexico, Texas was its own country for
several years before it became part of the United States in 1845.*

Famous Figures

SAM HOUSTON
(1793–1863)

Sam Houston was a Tennessee lawyer and politician before moving to Texas in 1832. He was a good friend of President Andrew Jackson, who was also from Tennessee. During the revolution of 1835 and 1836, Houston emerged as the commander in chief of the Texas army. He was elected as the first president of the Republic of Texas, holding that position until 1838 and again from 1841 to 1844. After Texas joined the Union, he served as a U.S. senator from 1846 to 1859. As governor of the state in 1861, Houston was forced out of office because he opposed Texas's leaving the Union to join the Confederacy, the group of Southern slave states that opposed the election of Abraham Lincoln.

Foreign Relations Issues

Many Texans hoped that the United States would officially recognize Texas as an independent nation and then annex it—add it to the Union. President Andrew Jackson accepted the idea that Texas had been part of the Louisiana Purchase. He and many members of his party, the Democrats, wanted to annex Texas and acquire other western lands, as well.

Jackson had already tried unsuccessfully to buy Texas from Mexico. Now, however, he was reluctant to annex the new Republic of Texas. The United States and Mexico had recently signed a trade treaty, and Jackson did not want to risk a war with the Mexicans. The president also worried that other nations would accuse the United States of violating international law by recognizing Texas, since Santa Anna claimed that it was still part of his country. Hoping to avoid these possible problems, Jackson decided against annexation. He also waited to recognize Texas's independence until March 1837, just before he left office.

Fast Fact

During the early nineteenth century, some Americans, acting without official government approval, invaded Texas and tried to take parts of it by force. This practice was called filibustering.

The new president, Martin Van Buren, also wanted to avoid the annexation issue. During Van Buren's one term as president, some Texans and Americans pushed for annexation, but he resisted. A growing number of Americans opposed annexation, and Van Buren didn't want to upset them. The next two presidents, William Henry Harrison and John Tyler, also hesitated to annex Texas. Both men belonged to the Whig Party, which in general did not favor westward expansion. Tyler, however, changed his mind in 1843. He wanted to expand the borders of the country, and he believed most Texans wanted annexation. He said that he saw "no sufficient reason to avoid...an act esteemed to be so desirable by both" Texas and himself.

Tyler, a former Democrat from Virginia, also supported the interests of the Southern states, and most Southerners wanted Texas in the Union, since slavery was legal there. For several decades, Northern members of Congress had been trying to limit the spread of slavery. Southerners wanted each new state to have the right to choose whether or not to allow slavery. The South feared that if the country had more free states than slave states, Congress would one day completely end slavery. Texas would give the nation one more slave state.

Foreign relations with Great Britain also influenced Tyler's thinking. The British, who had recognized Texas's independence in 1840, did not want the republic to become part of the United States. They hoped that an independent Texas might limit America's expansion westward at a time when the British still had an interest in western lands along the Pacific Coast. The British also hoped to buy Texas cotton at lower prices than the cotton it bought from Southern states. Knowing that an independent Texas served British interests, Tyler was eager to use annexation to stop the rival nation's plans.

> *Fast Fact*
>
> Sworn in as president in March 1841, William Henry Harrison served for only one month before dying of pneumonia, a lung disease. John Tyler then became the first person serving as vice president to step up to the presidency.

Struggles for Annexation

In 1844, Tyler began negotiating a treaty with Texas for annexation. Under the treaty, the U.S. government agreed to pay Texas's debts and protect its citizens. In return, all of Texas's lands would become part of the United States. Under the Constitution, all treaties with foreign countries must be approved by two-thirds of the U.S. Senate. By this time, antislavery groups had increased their opposition to annexation, since they did not want Texas to enter the Union as a slave state. These groups influenced the Senate to reject the annexation treaty.

At the end of 1844, before he turned over the presidency to James K. Polk, Tyler tried again to annex Texas. This time, he called for a joint resolution, or a statement from both the Senate and the House, calling for annexation. With a joint resolution, Tyler needed only majority approval of his plan, as opposed to two-thirds. The House approved the resolution, but the Senate was still divided. Some senators wanted to negotiate a new treaty with Texas. In the end, the Senate accepted a resolution that let the president choose either to accept the old treaty or to negotiate a new one. The resolution was approved on March 6, 1845, two days after Polk took office. He accepted the old treaty, and this time, the Senate approved it. The annexation deal was completed that summer, and on December 29, 1845, Texas was formally admitted as the twenty-eighth state.

A MAJOR ELECTION ISSUE

Annexation of Texas was one of the key issues as the Democrats and the Whigs chose candidates for the 1844 presidential election. Although Tyler had been elected as a Whig, his views were more Democratic, so the Whigs rejected him and chose Henry Clay. In general, the Whigs opposed annexation, and Clay did, too, but during the campaign, he seemed to change his position. He wrote that he favored acquiring Texas, as long as it was done peacefully. That stance upset Northern Whigs who opposed annexation in any form. The Democrats' candidate in 1844, James K. Polk, welcomed annexation and westward expansion in general. Polk defeated Clay in a fairly close election.

The Democrats Call for Annexation

The strongest supporters of annexation were Southern Democrats. They listed a number of reasons why acquiring Texas would be good for the United States. One reason was economic. If Texas were a state, more Americans and immigrants would settle in the region. They would create a new market for goods produced in the other states. Extending the country's borders in the region would also make it easier for Americans to trade with Mexico.

To some Democrats, annexation was really an issue of "reannexation." They believed that Texas had been part of the country once before, after the Louisiana Purchase. Taking back what had once been part of the United States was only fair. Senator Robert Walker of Mississippi held this view. In 1844, he wrote that Americans were merely "pursuing our ancient and rightful boundary."

Other Democrats emphasized the geographical and military importance of annexation. With control of Texas, the United States would then control several important western rivers and the Gulf of Mexico. That would give the United States an advantage in its effort to limit British actions in the West. In 1843, Andrew Jackson expressed his views on this issue in a private letter, which was later published. The former president feared that Great Britain would form an alliance with an independent Texas. Then the British could easily send troops to Texas and use them to attack the United States. If America annexed Texas, however, the country would have the Rio Grande as its western boundary. Jackson called the river and the area around it a natural defensive barrier against attack. He also suggested that the British could stir up slave revolts in the South if they had a military base in Texas. Annexation would limit that threat.

Slavery was a key part of the annexation issue for Southern slave owners. They thought that if Texas remained independent, British abolitionists would try to end slavery there. American abolitionists, who wanted an immediate end to slavery, were already active in the United States. The end of slavery in Texas might fuel the spread of abolitionist ideas in America.

Secretary of State John C. Calhoun was devoted to preserving slavery in the South. He wrote a letter to a British diplomat explaining that slavery was "essential

Fast Fact

Calhoun's letter to the British became public, and its proslavery statements angered Northern lawmakers. The letter contributed to the defeat of the annexation treaty of 1844.

to the peace, safety, and prosperity of those states of the Union in which it exists." The country could not stand for any outside threat that might weaken slavery. By annexing Texas, the United States would limit Britain's ability to influence the abolitionists' efforts.

In Their Own Words

Here is part of Robert Walker's *A Letter Relative to the Annexation of Texas,* expressing his views on the issue.

This is no question of the purchase of new territory, but of the reannexation of that which was once all our own.... It proposes no new addition to the valley of the Mississippi [river] but of its reunion, and all its waters once more under our dominion. If the Creator had separated Texas from the Union by mountain barriers, the Alps or the Andes, these might be plausible objections; but he has planned down the whole valley, including Texas...for the dominion of one government and the residence of one people.

Against Annexation

The Whig Party and some Northern Democrats led the opposition to annexation. Some had constitutional concerns. Daniel Webster, a leading Whig lawmaker and former secretary of state, argued that the government could buy land from a foreign country, as the United States had done with Louisiana in 1803. However, the Constitution did not give Congress or the president the legal right to add a new country to the Union's territory.

Some Whigs opposed annexation because they feared a war with Mexico. During most of the debate over annexation, the Mexicans still claimed Texas as part of their country. If Mexico chose to fight for Texas, newspaper editor Theodore Sedgwick Jr.

wrote, a war would lead to "ruinous expense and destruction to commerce." Sedgwick also said that the United States could not afford a war after just spending tens of millions of dollars to resettle Native American tribes from the Southeast to lands west of the Mississippi River.

For most Whigs, the problem with annexation came down to one key issue: slavery. Abolitionists wanted to end slavery everywhere, because they hated the pain and loss of freedom that slaves endured, and because it was against their own religious beliefs. Whigs who were not abolitionists still opposed adding new slave states. They hoped that, over time, a majority of lawmakers in free states would vote in Congress to end slavery across the country. If Texas entered the Union as a slave state, it would likely elect U.S. representatives and senators who would support the continued expansion of slavery into other new territories and states. The debate over limiting or allowing slavery in new states had already sparked heated arguments in Congress and in newspapers across the country. Some Whigs feared that annexing Texas would renew the argument and possibly lead to dissolution—the splitting of the North and South into separate countries.

Despite these arguments, the lawmakers who favored slavery and the country's growth won the annexation issue. However, the debate over the future of slavery in America was not over.

> ### Fast Fact
> Daniel Webster resigned as President Tyler's secretary of state in May 1843 because Tyler pursued policies that did not reflect Whig beliefs. Webster's replacement, Abel Upshur, strongly supported annexing Texas.

Daniel Webster, in 1845.

In Their Own Words

Here is part of a statement signed by thirteen members of Congress opposing the annexation of Texas.

[Annexation] would be...an attempt to [make permanent] an institution...so unjust...so injurious to the interests and abhorrent to the feelings of the people of the free states, as...to result in a dissolution of the Union...and we not only assert that the people of the free states ought not to submit to it, but we say, with confidence, THEY WOULD NOT SUBMIT TO IT.

CHAPTER FOUR

The Mexican War

WHAT
The United States goes to war with Mexico.

ISSUES
*The need for war to settle issues between the two countries; the
desire of some Americans for westward expansion*

WHERE
Nationwide

WHEN
1846–1848

*I*n 1845, the United States annexed, or took control of, the Republic of Texas. Just ten years earlier, Texas had been part of Mexico. The region was dominated by white American settlers—many of them slave owners—who, in 1835 and 1836, led a revolution that won Texas's independence from Mexico. From the beginning, most Texans believed that, one day, their new country would be part of the United States, and many Americans welcomed the addition of Texas to the Union.

The annexation of Texas upset Mexican leaders, who had still considered Texas part of their country after it became an independent republic in 1836. They didn't want to see Texas as an independent nation, but they wanted even less to see it as part of the United States. The Mexican government therefore only recognized Texas's independence in 1845, in a last attempt to stop the annexation. Mexicans hoped that the Texans would choose to stay independent if they did not have to fear Mexico's trying to reclaim their land. Most Texans, however, were eager to join the United States.

Once the annexation deal was complete, Mexico was angry that the United States considered the Rio Grande the border between Texas and Mexico. Most people—including many Texans—had accepted the Nueces River as the legal border. Few Texans had ever settled in the region between the two rivers. Still, President James Polk wanted the Rio Grande as the border. At the same time, he eyed further U.S. expansion into Mexican lands, especially California. Polk, like many Americans of the era, believed in what was sometimes called Manifest Destiny. This was the idea that the expansion of the United States could not be prevented and was not only just, but almost an obligation placed upon Americans by God. The phrase

Fast Fact

The Rio Grande, at 1,900 miles (3,040 kilometers), is one of the longest rivers in North America. It lies about 100 miles (160 kilometers) south of the Nueces River, which starts in southwestern Texas and flows into the Gulf of Mexico.

describes a general mood rather than a precise policy, because the limits to this expansion were never officially set.

In the fall of 1845, Polk sent John Slidell, a congressional representative from Louisiana, to Mexico to discuss the border issue. The United States also wanted the Mexicans to pay money that some Texans claimed they were owed. In addition, Polk told Slidell to try to buy California and New Mexico from the Mexicans. Slidell never had the chance—the Mexicans refused to deal with him. They were still angry over the annexation and the presence of U.S. troops in what they considered their land. Polk had already sent U.S. troops to Corpus Christi, a town just south of the Nueces River. When Slidell's talks failed, the president ordered the troops in Corpus Christi to move closer to the Rio Grande.

The War Begins

Under the command of General Zachary Taylor, the Americans built a camp near the Rio Grande, across from the Mexican town of Matamoros. By April 1846, the Mexicans had about 5,000 troops in the town, while Taylor commanded about 3,000. Most historians believe that Polk was trying to start a war by threatening the Mexicans. On April 25, he got his wish when Mexican and U.S. troops clashed just outside Matamoros.

Even before he learned about this battle, Polk was preparing to go to war with Mexico. Polk was upset that the Mexicans had refused to deal with Slidell and accept the Rio Grande as the U.S.-Mexico border. He also still wanted more Mexican lands. Polk told his cabinet, "We must...take a bold and firm course toward Mexico." When he finally heard from Taylor about the fighting, Polk sought the support of Congress for a war against Mexico. Because Polk's Democratic Party controlled the House of Representatives and the Senate, he won the approval that he sought for the war. Still, some Democrats joined the Whigs, members of the other major party, in opposing the war.

Despite strong debates in Congress, most Americans favored the war—at least in the beginning. They accepted Polk's version of the situation: The Rio Grande was the true border, and Mexican troops had "invaded our territory and shed American blood upon the American soil." Across the country, 60,000 young men eagerly volunteered to fight in Mexico, crying "Mexico or Death!" Over time, more Americans spoke out against the war, though it remained popular with residents in the South and West.

Famous Figures

ZACHARY TAYLOR
(1784–1850)

Thanks to the Mexican War (1846–1848), Zachary Taylor became a national hero—and the twelfth president of the United States. With the help of his second cousin, President James Madison, Taylor became an officer in the U.S. Army in 1808. During the War of 1812 (1812–1815), he defended an Indiana fort from Native American attacks. After the war, he briefly retired from the military and then returned to duty in 1819. During the Mexican War, he won a major victory when his troops defeated a much larger Mexican force at Buena Vista. In 1848, the Whig Party nominated him as its presidential candidate. Although he had never served in politics, Taylor won because of his war record. He was often called "Old Rough and Ready" because of his bluntness and preference for civilian clothes to a uniform, even in battle. He died in office in 1850.

Victory and Growth

As Polk prepared for war, Taylor won several battles in northern Mexico. At the same time, a small U.S. force captured Santa Fe, New Mexico. In California, American residents had already proclaimed their territory to be an independent country. U.S. troops then helped the rebels fight off Mexicans who resisted American control.

In March 1847, a U.S. Army Regiment led by General Winfield Scott landed at Vera Cruz, Mexico, and headed for Mexico City, the capital. By the fall, the Americans controlled Mexico City, and the Mexicans were ready to discuss peace. On February 2, 1848, the two sides signed the Treaty of Guadeloupe-Hidalgo. Mexico agreed to recognize the Rio Grande as the border with Texas. It also officially handed over California, New Mexico, and other western lands to the United States—these lands would

At the Battle of Buena Vista, pictured here, future president Zachary "Old Rough and Ready" Taylor distinguished himself as a fearless military leader. In that 1847 battle, he led a force of Americans that was outnumbered almost four to one to a stunning victory against Mexican general Santa Anna and his troops.

later become states. The U.S. government paid Mexico $15 million and agreed to pay any claims that Americans had against Mexico. With the treaty, the United States added more than 500,000 square miles (1.3 million square kilometers) of new territory.

Some Americans were not satisfied with those gains. They suggested that the country should take all of Mexico. However, most Americans thought that it was better to let some of Mexico stay independent. They did not want to have to govern a foreign people—the Mexicans. Some Americans also thought that the United States had done the right thing by paying for the new territory. That move, one newspaper wrote, would "lay a broad foundation for future harmony" with Mexico.

The Arguments for War

On one level, Polk and many Americans saw the Mexican War as a defensive war. If the Rio Grande were the border between the United States and Mexico, as Polk claimed, then the Mexicans had invaded U.S. territory. The Americans had the right to protect their borders from foreign armies.

Polk noted that trouble had been growing between the two countries since the annexation issue. The Mexican government had refused to pay the money that it owed Texans and to talk with American diplomats. Other Democrats claimed that, for years, Mexico had taken actions that threatened the United States. One Democratic newspaper wrote in 1847, "We have borne our wrongs from her with patience, until patience has ceased to be a virtue." Sending troops across the Rio Grande and firing on U.S. troops was just the last in a string of Mexican insults.

However, Manifest Destiny explained Polk's real reasons for fighting the war with Mexico. He and many Americans wanted to expand into New Mexico and California. To some people, acquiring Mexican lands was a racial—and racist—issue. They believed that white people of English background were superior to Mexicans and that Manifest Destiny reflected the fact that Americans were chosen to rule in order to spread their culture to new lands. As one naval officer wrote after the war, Americans had been placed next to "an inferior people, in order, without a doubt, that we may sweep over them, and remove them (as a people) and their worn-out institutions from the face of the earth."

In Their Own Words

Here is part of James Polk's message to Congress, calling for war with Mexico.

I had ordered an efficient military force to take a position "between the Nueces and the [Rio Grande]." This had become necessary to meet [an]...invasion of Texas by the Mexican forces...threatened solely because Texas had determined...to annex herself to our Union, and under these circumstances it was plainly our duty to extend our protection over her citizens and soil....

As war exists...by the act of Mexico herself, we are called upon by every consideration of duty and patriotism to vindicate with decision the honor, the rights, and the interests of our country.

Fierce Opposition to the War

Although many average Americans supported the war, a diverse group of politicians and reformers opposed it. The loudest protests came from Whigs and from New Englanders who opposed slavery. The antislavery forces believed that Polk and the Democrats wanted to acquire more land for the country so that they could spread slavery into new states.

> *Fast Fact*
>
> The Mexican War was sometimes called "Mr. Polk's War."

In Congress, Polk's critics accused him of trying to force Mexico into a war without the United States actually declaring one. They argued that the Nueces, not the Rio Grande, was the accepted border between the two countries. Sending U.S. troops into the disputed territory was meant to spark a war. Garrett Davis, a Whig from Kentucky, said, "Our own president...began this war. He had been carrying it on for months." Antiwar Whigs said that Polk could have continued to try diplomacy to settle problems with Mexico. Instead, Polk chose a path that seemed likely to lead to war.

Some Whigs also disliked how Polk presented the war to Congress. He did not ask it to declare war, as only Congress can under the U.S. Constitution. Instead, he said that war already existed and asked Congress to approve sending supplies and troops. If the members refused, they were likely to be called unpatriotic for not supporting the president and the military when the country was under attack.

A few Whigs opposed going to war with Mexico because they feared that it might harm the United States' relations with Great Britain. The British had opposed the annexation of Texas and, in general, did not want the United States to expand and gain more power. Great Britain and the United States had also been arguing over the border between the United States and Canada in the Northwest. The war with Mexico might threaten the deal that the two sides had just reached, or the British might step in and help the Mexicans.

Several Democrats joined the Whigs in protesting the war. The best known was John C. Calhoun of South Carolina. He, like some Whigs, believed that war could have been avoided through diplomacy, and he disliked Polk's attempt to force Congress to declare war. He thought that Polk was trying to claim Congress's legal power to declare war. "It sets the example," he wrote, "which will enable all future Presidents to bring about a state of things, in which Congress shall be forced...to declare war."

Just as some Americans used racist views to argue for conquest, antiwar forces also raised race as an issue. Some of Polk's opponents did not want the United States to take over land where supposedly inferior people lived. In addition, most Mexicans were Roman Catholic. U.S. political and business leaders were largely Protestant and did not like the Catholic Church, a historical hatred with roots in old religious conflicts with Catholics. Some Americans did not want Mexican Catholics living in U.S. territory.

The various arguments against the Mexican War and against the acquisition of new territory did not hurt Polk's efforts. In the end, he achieved most of what he wanted. In the future, however, some Americans would make similar arguments in opposing other foreign wars.

The arguments against the Mexican War were many and diverse. Despite these protests, President Polk achieved most of what he wanted from the war: adding vast amounts of land to the United States. In this 1848 cartoon, people come to Polk to solve their problems concerning Mexico.

In Their Own Words

Charles Sumner was an abolitionist—someone who demanded an immediate end to slavery across the United States. After the Mexican War he served as a U.S. senator from Massachusetts. Here is part of an article that he wrote in 1847 against the Mexican War.

As a war of conquest, and for the extension of slavery, [the war] is contrary to the principles of the Constitution, which…was formed "to provide for the common defense, promote the general welfare, and secure the blessings of liberty to ourselves and our posterity." Such a war as that in which we are now engaged…is not for the common defense, nor to secure the blessings of liberty.

CHAPTER FIVE

The Seneca Falls Convention

WHAT

The United States holds its first major convention to discuss equal rights for women.

ISSUE

The role of women in U.S. politics and society

WHERE

Seneca Falls, New York

WHEN

1848

*T*hrough colonial times and the first half of the nine-teenth century, women had almost no legal rights in America. Men dominated all parts of life: politics, social organizations, and the economy. Men—and many women—thought that men and women were not equal and that women lacked the intelligence and other qualities needed to be independent.

During the eighteenth century, a few women protested against the inequality that women suffered. In 1776, Abigail Adams, wife of future president John Adams, told her husband that she and other women "will not hold ourselves bound by any laws in which we have no voice, or representation." John Adams and the other male leaders rejected this notion. After the American Revolution (1775–1783), Judith Sargent Stevens Murray wrote several articles favoring the equality of men and women—at least as far as their intelligence was concerned. Murray's ideas were not widely accepted.

For decades, the only group that challenged the notion of sexual inequality was the Society of Friends. The members of this religious organization were called Quakers. Unlike women in other churches in America, Quaker women preached and held leadership positions. This concern for equality, however, did not spread outside of Quaker society until the nine-teenth century. Individual Quakers played key roles in organizing the first women's movement—the effort to gain equal rights for women.

Fast Fact

Many reformers during the Second Great Awakening tried to convince Americans to reduce the amount of alcohol that they drank or quit drinking altogether. This effort was known as the temperance movement.

From Antislavery to Women's Rights

During the early nineteenth century, America went through what is called "the Second Great Awakening." The First Great Awakening, which began in the 1740s, had called for people to live by the teachings of the Bible and accept Jesus Christ as their savior. The ministers who called for this religious "awakening" thought that traditional ministers placed too much stress on reason and not enough on faith and emotion. The Second Great Awakening was a second attempt to make Christianity a stronger force in American life. As during the First Great Awakening, ministers traveled across the country to give sermons and find people willing to confess their sins and accept Jesus.

Many well-educated people who were influenced by the Second Great Awakening wanted to reform society—for example, by improving public education and aiding charities. In the North, some people known as abolitionists also called for an immediate end to slavery.

William Lloyd Garrison was the leading American abolitionist of the 1830s. He welcomed women into the antislavery movement, but other men were not ready to accept women in their abolitionist organizations. In addition, male leaders only let female abolitionists speak to audiences of women. Throughout America at this time, women usually were not allowed to speak in public in front of men.

Two sisters from South Carolina, Sarah Grimké and Angelina Grimké Weld, argued that women abolitionists had a right to speak in public. Their desire to play an active role in ending slavery led them to advocate equality for women. Weld wrote, "What then can *woman* do for the slave, when she herself is under the feet of *man* and shamed into silence?"

> *Fast Fact*
>
> In 1840, Garrison was one of the leaders of the American Anti-Slavery Society. That year, the group split apart. One of the issues that upset some members was Garrison's call for equal rights for women.

The Road to Seneca Falls

In 1840, several American women attended the World Anti-Slavery Convention, held in London, England. Except for William Lloyd Garrison and a few others, the men who ran the convention did not want the women to take part. In the end, the women were allowed to stay in the convention hall, but they had to sit by themselves behind a curtain.

Two of the American women at the convention were Lucretia Mott and Elizabeth Cady Stanton. Mott, a Quaker, was one of the leading female abolitionists. In London, she became friends with Stanton, who had come to the convention with her husband, Henry. The treatment that the women received at the convention angered Stanton and turned her attention to women's rights. She and Mott decided that when they returned to the United States, they would form a society to work for female equality.

Stanton spent the next several years raising a family, which limited her work for women's rights. Finally, in 1848, she and Mott organized a convention to discuss women's political issues. They held it in Seneca Falls, New York, where Stanton was living at the time.

The Seneca Falls Convention opened on July 19. On the first day, about 100 people attended, including some men curious about the meeting. Stanton announced, "We have met here today to discuss our rights and wrongs, civil and political." A few days before, Stanton had written "A Declaration of Rights and Sentiments." Borrowing some of the wording of the Declaration of Independence, she spelled out the women's complaints and their ideas on equality.

On the second day, the convention drew 300 people. After a long day of speeches, 100 of them—sixty-eight women and thirty-two men—signed the Declaration of Rights and Sentiments. The audience was mostly local people, but news of the convention soon spread across the country.

In general, ministers and newspaper editors attacked the convention and its goals. Despite the criticism, Stanton and other reformers were committed to women's rights. Similar conventions were held in other towns, and women met at a national convention in Worcester, Massachusetts, in 1850. Stanton did not attend, but she sent a letter that was read to more than 1,000 people. Over the next fifteen years, however, the women's movement grew slowly. Reformers and politicians were more concerned about slavery and the threat of a civil war.

At the time of the Seneca Falls Convention, the idea of women speaking publicly about anything, let alone women's rights, was virtually unheard of and unacceptable to many people. In this illustration, Lucretia Mott, one of the organizers of the convention, is protected from an angry male mob.

ELIZABETH CADY STANTON
(1815–1902)

Elizabeth Cady Stanton, along with Susan B. Anthony, was the leader of the first national women's movement in the United States. Stanton was born outside Albany, New York. She was already interested in social reform when she married abolitionist Henry Stanton. In her work for women's rights, Stanton upset many Americans by demanding that women receive suffrage, or the right to vote. She met Anthony in 1851, and the two worked together on this issue for decades. In addition to promoting women's suffrage, Stanton called for women to use birth control and to divorce husbands who treated them poorly. Her stance on these issues weakened her support in the women's movement. Most women were still not ready to embrace those positions.

The Defense of Women's Rights

Supporters of the women's movement, like abolitionists, used both religious and political beliefs in their fight for equality. Quakers believed that everyone was equal in God's eyes, in both religious and practical matters, and that God did not expect women to serve men or be under their control.

Stanton and others in the women's movement were more likely to point to the ideas that had shaped the Declaration of Independence, especially in the struggle for suffrage. Americans believed in the idea of natural rights—rights that all humans had in their natural state, before forming societies. These rights included life, liberty, and property. Women and men had the same natural rights. Since political rights were based on natural rights, women should have the same political rights as men.

Some men, including future U.S. president Abraham Lincoln, were willing to accept that women who met the voting requirements should be given suffrage. During the 1820s and 1830s, Americans in general wanted to expand democracy and give more people the right to vote. Stanton and others argued that all women should have that right. Stanton noted that "drunkards, idiots... [and] rowdies" could vote—as long as they were men. She thought that it was reasonable to give women suffrage, since they were by nature equal and since many women were actually more qualified to vote than some of the drunkards and idiots.

In her letters of the 1830s, Sarah Grimké outlined the qualities of women that showed their equality. She argued that women were just as intelligent as men, even though men tried to deny them the chance to learn by keeping them out of universities. She also discussed women in history who had shown the same heroism as men. Grimké wanted to show "that our views about the duties of men and the duties of women, the sphere of man and the sphere of woman, are mere arbitrary opinions, differing in different ages and countries."

Fast Fact

In general, the early women's movement focused on equal rights for white women, though some free African American women did join the movement. One of the most important was Sojourner Truth, a former slave who also supported the abolitionist movement.

RARE RIGHTS IN NEW JERSEY

For thirty years, New Jersey was the only place in the United States where women could vote. In 1776, the state created a constitution that allowed all free residents who owned property to vote. Most states specifically said that only free males (or free white males) could vote. However, few women actually voted in New Jersey elections until 1790, when the state government made it clear that single women who owned property were allowed to vote. (Since husbands took legal control of their wives' property, the state constitution never allowed married women to vote.) A Quaker named Joseph Cooper led the effort to spell out the voting rights of single women. In 1807, after some women used their political power and almost defeated a male candidate, New Jersey took away the women's right to vote.

In Their Own Words

Here is part of the Declaration of Rights and Sentiments, written by Elizabeth Cady Stanton and approved at the 1848 Seneca Falls Convention.

We hold these truths to be self-evident: that all men and women are created equal; that they are endowed by their Creator with certain inalienable rights; that among these are life, liberty, and the pursuit of happiness....

The history of mankind is a history of repeated injuries...on the part of man toward woman, having in direct object the establishment of an absolute tyranny over her....

We insist that [women] have immediate admission to all the rights and privileges which belong to them as citizens of the United States.

Attacks on the Women's Movement

The most vocal opponents of the women's movement were ministers and politicians. Many Protestants of the era believed that the Bible gave men authority over women. Politicians turned to English common law to argue for men's dominance over women. This system of law, which had been developed through court cases in England over hundreds of years, formed the foundation for the U.S. legal system.

To the ministers, God had clearly meant for women to serve men. According to the Bible, they said, women gave up their rights to men and in exchange received protection and help meeting their basic needs. Some ministers pointed specifically to Genesis, the first book in the Bible, which states that God created man (Adam) first and then created woman (Eve) from a part of him—his rib. The ministers claimed that this showed that man was more important to God than woman.

Later books of the Bible had specific rules about what women could and could not do. Saint Paul said that women could not speak in church. American men of the era thought this meant that women should not speak publicly at all, and certainly not on important matters such as politics.

Many American men believed that women had only certain roles to play in society. The most important was being a wife and mother. In general, women could also do charity work and some religious activities. However, as one religious group claimed during the 1830s, women who wanted the same powers as men were "unnatural." After the Seneca Falls Convention, some critics suggested that the women seeking equal rights were trying to reverse the traditional roles of men and women. That effort, they claimed, would destroy the family as God had created it.

Fast Fact

In 1890, Wyoming entered the Union as a suffragist state— women had the right to vote in state and local elections. Five more states— Colorado, Idaho, Utah, Washington, and California—gave women the right to vote before 1920, when all American women were granted that right by the Nineteenth Amendment to the Constitution.

The religious basis for inequality carried over into English common law. The Bible said that the husband was the head of the household. Common law—and American attitudes—reflected the thinking of William Blackstone, an English legal scholar, who wrote, "The very being or legal existence of woman is suspended during marriage." A married woman's legal and political interests were represented by her husband. Young single women were supposedly represented by their fathers or other male relatives. The fact that some single women did own property was not considered important enough to justify granting them political rights—particularly the right to vote.

For decades, suffrage remained the most controversial issue of the women's movement. Some male politicians felt threatened by the idea of women having political power, since it would mean that the men would have to give up some of the power that they enjoyed. American women did not receive the right to vote in national elections until 1920.

In Their Own Words

A Philadelphia, Pennsylvania, newspaper, *The Public Ledger and Daily Transcript,* was one of many papers that criticized the Seneca Falls Convention. Here is part of what the paper wrote.

Women have enough influence over human affairs without being politicians. Is not everything managed by female influence? Mothers, grandmothers, aunts, and sweethearts manage everything. Men have nothing to do but to listen and obey to the "of course, my dear, you will, and of course, my dear, you won't." Their rule is absolute; their power unbounded. Under such a system men have no claim to rights, especially "equal rights."

A woman is nobody. A wife is everything. A pretty girl is equal to ten thousand men, and a mother is, next to God, all powerful.

CHAPTER SIX

The Compromise of 1850

WHAT

Congress passes a series of laws regarding slavery.

ISSUES

Extending slavery into new territories; preserving the Union

WHERE

Nationwide

WHEN

1850

With its victory in the Mexican War (1846–1848), the United States acquired more than 500,000 square miles (1.3 million square kilometers) of new territory. The most prized region was California, with its valuable ports on the Pacific Ocean. The new land, however, brought up an old issue: whether or not states formed in new U.S. territories should be allowed to permit slavery.

The debate over extending slavery had first come up in 1820, in Missouri. Missouri had been part of the Louisiana Purchase, a large part of North America that the United States bought from France in 1803. Slavery had been legal there under French rule, and it remained legal when Missouri became a U.S. territory. In 1820, Missouri sought to enter the Union as a state. Northern lawmakers wanted to place limits on slavery in Missouri as a condition for its becoming a state. Southerners, who generally favored the expansion of slavery, were against any limits.

While Missouri was trying to enter the Union, Maine was also seeking statehood. Slavery was illegal there. Members of Congress argued over the bills that would allow the two states to enter the Union. The lawmakers finally decided that Maine would enter as a free state and Missouri would enter as a slave state. In addition, Congress limited the spread of slavery in other western lands that had been part of the Louisiana Purchase. An imaginary line drawn westward from the southern border of Missouri would mark the divide. Above the line, slavery would be outlawed; below it, a territory had the right to allow slavery. This "Missouri Compromise" of 1820 ended the debate over the spread of slavery—for a while.

By the 1840s, slavery was once again a heated issue between the North and South. The abolitionist movement grew during the 1830s. Abolitionists, who were mostly Northerners,

Fast Fact

In 1849, the United States had thirty states equally divided between slave and free.

demanded an immediate end to slavery across the country. Their opponents had a variety of views. Some believed that it was up to each state to decide whether or not slavery was legal. Others disliked slavery but thought that it should end over time, as older slaves were freed or died and slave owners did not replace them. The most vocal supporters of slavery wanted it to spread westward so that new states would elect congressional representatives who would fight the abolitionists. At the least, proslavery forces wanted an equal number of slave states and free states.

CALIFORNIA GOLD

Soon after the United States signed the treaty that ended the Mexican War, Americans learned that California was even more valuable than they had imagined. Gold was discovered there in January 1848, setting off the huge "gold rush" that brought 200,000 people to California in just a few years. Miners came from all over world, especially China, the eastern United States, and Europe. Few of the new arrivals made the fortunes that they dreamed about, but they boosted California's economy throughout the nineteenth century.

Slave or Free?

In 1849, California asked to enter the Union. Normally, it would have had to become a U.S. territory first, but its population and economy had boomed, thanks to the gold rush. President Zachary Taylor suggested that both California and New Mexico enter the Union. Under Mexican rule, neither region had allowed slavery, so they planned to enter the Union as free states.

Taylor's plan angered proslavery Southerners. They realized that most of the lands from the Louisiana Purchase, as well as the Oregon Territory in the Northwest, would become free states. The lands won from Mexico might be their last hope for adding new slave states and getting more proslavery representatives in Congress. Even then, much of that region was not suited for growing cotton, the main crop in the slave states. California was the most likely place for a new slave state. Adding California and New Mexico as free states, furthermore, would upset the current balance between slave and free states.

Some Southerners suggested that the old boundary line from the Missouri Compromise be extended to the Pacific Ocean. Then slavery would be allowed in at least part of California. Other Southerners wanted a new fugitive slave law, to make it easier for slave owners to capture runaway slaves and punish people who helped them escape.

The plan to admit California and New Mexico as free states led to a great debate in Congress. Members of the Free-Soil Party had their own proposals on slavery. They wanted to end the slave trade and slavery itself in Washington, D.C. Robert Toombs, a Southerner in the House of Representatives, responded that "if by your legislation you seek to drive us from the territories of California and New Mexico...and to abolish slavery in this District...*I am for disunion.*"

Disunion, or splitting up the country into two separate nations, was a heated topic at the time. During the past two decades, both abolitionists and slave owners had occasionally said that the North and South would be better off splitting apart. In 1844, the American Anti-Slavery Society called for disunion, arguing that the U.S. Constitution promoted slavery and that the North would be better off pursuing disunion and drafting a new constitution. Wendell Phillips, a leading abolitionist, expressed this view when he wrote, "No union with slaveholders!" On the other side, Representative Toombs was just the latest of several Southerners who had talked of disunion.

The views for and against slavery in the North and South grew stronger every year. However, most politicians wanted to preserve the Union at all costs. They believed that Congress could find another compromise over slavery, just as it had in 1820. That year, Henry Clay of Kentucky had led the fight for a compromise. In 1850, he once again pursued a plan that would settle the argument without disunion.

Fast Fact
In 1850, Henry Clay was serving in the U.S. Senate for the fourth time.

The fugitive slave law, a key part of the Compromise of 1850, said that citizens were obligated to help capture runaway slaves. In this 1851 scene, the police line the docks as they watch the departure of slave Thomas Sims on the Acorn. After a brief trial, the police had escorted the fugitive slave Sims to the ship and sent him back to Georgia. The police ensured that the law was upheld and that abolitionists would not be able to "kidnap" Sims.

The Compromise of 1850

Clay talked with Senator Daniel Webster of Massachusetts, who opposed the spread of slavery, and with some Southerners who wanted to preserve the Union. Then on January 29, he introduced a series of laws that he hoped would appeal to lawmakers from both the North and the South. Both sides would have to accept some laws that they did not like in order to approve the entire package.

Clay said that California should enter the Union as a free state. New Mexico and Utah would become territories, with no mention of slavery. Two points of Clay's compromise involved Texas, which had a dispute with New Mexico over their shared border. Southerners favored Texas's claim to New Mexican territory because, as a slave state, Texas could expand slavery into those lands. Clay proposed that the federal government should give Texas money in exchange for Texas giving up its claims in New Mexico. The government would also pay some of Texas's old debts.

The plan proposed ending the slave trade in Washington, D.C., but not slavery itself—people would not be able to buy and sell slaves there, but they could still own them. Maryland, which bordered the District of Columbia on three sides, would have to approve any plan to end slavery in the capital. Clay also said that Congress should pass a tougher fugitive slave law, as Southern slave owners wanted, and that Congress should not interfere in the slave trade between the states.

Both Northerners and Southerners saw problems with Clay's compromise. Still, Clay convinced them to combine all the parts of the plan into one bill, and he won support for it. Then, after months of debate, the Senate decided to split the plan into separate bills. That way, senators could choose which parts to accept or reject. They also made changes to some parts.

Fast Fact

In general, President Taylor approved of the aims of Clay's compromise. However, Taylor never saw the compromise become law, because he died suddenly in July 1850. The new president, Millard Fillmore, also accepted the compromise plan.

For example, one bill specified that New Mexico and Utah would decide on their own whether or not to accept slavery. As separate bills, the plan passed and became law.

THE FUGITIVE SLAVE LAW OF 1850

The Fugitive Slave Law of 1850 was crucial for winning Southern support for the Compromise of 1850. Abolitionists, however, strongly condemned the new law. It gave the government the power to force civilians to help catch runaway slaves or face being fined or arrested. The new law also prevented accused runaways from arguing their cases before a jury or defending themselves in court. Some free blacks in the North were falsely accused of being slaves and sent into slavery in the South.

Arguments against the Compromise

The Compromise of 1850 emerged as the North and South continued to develop opposing views on slavery. This sectional division played a role in the debate over the compromise. Party politics also played a part. Taylor and Clay belonged to the Whig Party. Their major opponents, the Democrats, did not want to see either man gain political strength by achieving a compromise. In general, Southern Democrats led the attacks on the compromise, though some Northern Whigs also opposed it.

In the Senate, one leading opponent was John C. Calhoun of South Carolina. He saw the compromise as part of a growing pattern to deny slave owners the right to move into new territories with their slaves. Calhoun favored disunion if the South continued to lose its freedoms. When Whigs criticized the idea of disunion,

Fast Fact

Calhoun died in March 1850, before the final vote on the compromise. He left behind notes for a possible way to restructure the U.S. government. Calhoun proposed having two presidents—one for the North and one for the South. Both would have to approve any new laws passed by Congress.

Calhoun asserted, "The Union *can* be broken." Senator Jefferson Davis of Mississippi also condemned the compromise. He led the effort to extend the dividing line between slave and free states to the Pacific Ocean, which failed.

In the North, some Whigs and Free-Soilers opposed the compromise, because they thought that it did not do enough to limit slavery. William Seward, a senator from New York, said that the compromise was "radically wrong and essentially vicious" because slavery was a sin. The Fugitive Slave Law also came under fire, because it forced Northern whites to join posses and hunt for escaped slaves. Although the Compromise of 1850 passed, it upset people with extreme views on slavery—both for and against.

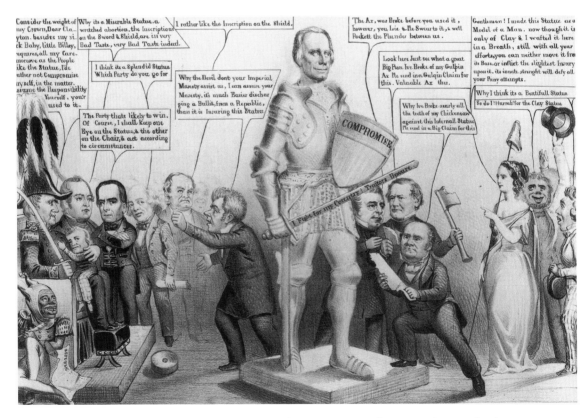

The main issue of the Compromise of 1850 was preserving the Union. Support for the compromise was widespread. In this cartoon, Henry Clay is a statue "Designed by the Goddess of Liberty" and supported, at right, by Liberty and the people.

THE WILMOT PROVISO

During the Mexican War, Pennsylvania lawmaker David Wilmot had called for a law that would prohibit slavery in any territory that the United States obtained from Mexico. This "Wilmot Proviso" passed the House of Representatives, but the Senate rejected it. Some Southerners claimed that the Compromise of 1850 was another attempt to put the same restrictions on slavery. Many of the senators who opposed the proviso also attacked the compromise.

In Their Own Words

Here is part of the speech that John C. Calhoun wrote in March 1850 against the compromise.

The South asks for justice, simple justice, and less she ought not to take. She has no compromise to offer but the Constitution, and no concession or surrender to make. She has already surrendered so much that she has little left to surrender....

...The North has only to...do justice by conceding to the South an equal right in the acquired territory...to cease the agitation of the slave question.

Supporting the Compromise

Clay, Webster, and others—mostly Northern Democrats and Southern Whigs—saw one major reason to support the compromise. Passing the laws would keep the Union together. These men believed that the radicals truly would seek disunion if they did not get their way.

Clay tried to counter some of the arguments both Northern and Southern opponents made against the compromise. Some Northerners wanted to add the specific language of the Wilmot Proviso regarding the spread of slavery in the West. Clay said that neither California nor New Mexico wanted slavery, so why stir up the South with a law that it detested? In New Mexico, he said, nature had already decided the issue. The region lacked the kind of farmland that would require slaves.

Clay was disappointed that his compromise was split into separate bills, but the move guaranteed that all would pass. Also helping his cause was the general mood of the country. The economy was strong, and most voters had not taken a strong position on the spread of slavery. Public opinion for and against slavery became louder in the years after the Compromise of 1850.

In Their Own Words

In July 1850, Henry Clay called for passing the compromise and preserving the Union. Here is part of what he said.

I believe from the bottom of my soul, that the measure is the re-union of this Union.... Let us forget popular fears, from whatever quarter they may spring. Let us...think alone of our God, our country, our consciences, and our glorious Union; that Union without which we shall be torn into hostile fragments, and sooner or later become the victims of military despotism, or foreign domination.

CHAPTER SEVEN

The Kansas-Nebraska Act

WHAT

Congress creates the territories of Kansas and Nebraska.

ISSUE

The expansion of slavery into new territories

WHERE

Kansas and Nebraska

WHEN

1854–1856

*D*uring the first half of the nineteenth century, Congress often debated whether to allow slavery in newly acquired territories and states entering the Union. Southern lawmakers generally favored the expansion of slavery, while many Northerners opposed it. By the 1850s, the issue was especially heated because antislavery feelings had grown in the North. Southerners, meanwhile, were convinced that they needed slavery to keep their plantations running smoothly. These large farms made up a major part of their economy.

Fast Fact

The line drawn to separate slave and free states in the West ran along a northern latitude that measured 36 degrees, 30 minutes.

In 1820, Congress had decided to limit slavery in the lands that formed the Louisiana Purchase, a large area west of the Mississippi River. The United States had bought Louisiana from France in 1803. Missouri, a new state carved out of the territory, was allowed to enter the Union as a slave state. At the same time, Maine joined as a free state. As part of the law letting these states enter the Union, an imaginary line drawn westward from the southern border of Missouri marked a dividing line for the future expansion of slavery in the West. Above the line, slavery would be outlawed; below it, a territory had the right to allow slavery. This arrangement was called the Missouri Compromise.

The issue of limiting slavery came up again in 1850. This time, the debate centered on the lands that the United States had acquired from Mexico in the Mexican War (1846–1848). In the end, Congress passed the Compromise of 1850. The law allowed California to enter the Union as a free state. In the territories of New Mexico and Utah, the citizens would have popular sover-eignty—they could decide on their own whether or not to accept slavery. Parts of New Mexico and all of Utah were north of the Missouri Compromise line.

A New Call for Expansion

At the beginning of 1854, Senator Stephen Douglas of Illinois hoped to create another new territory above the Missouri Compromise line. By law, the region, known as Nebraska, had to become a territory so that settlers could buy land from the government and move there. Douglas knew, however, that Southern lawmakers would oppose creating a new territory in Nebraska, which had been part of the Louisiana Purchase. Under the Missouri Compromise, slavery would be outlawed there.

To get around Southern opposition, Douglas suggested passing a law that would create two new territories. The first, Kansas, would be just west of Missouri and north of Oklahoma. The much larger Nebraska Territory would start at the northern border of Kansas, west of Iowa, and run to the Canadian border. Douglas also called for overturning the limits of the Missouri Compromise and allowing popular sovereignty in the new territories. Kansas, he assumed, would probably allow slavery, since it bordered the slave state of Missouri. The more northern territory of Nebraska would likely oppose slavery. In either case, the people themselves would decide, not Congress. Douglas said, "The great principle of self government is at stake."

Douglas also had political reasons for creating the Kansas-Nebraska Act. His party, the Democrats, controlled the White House and Congress. At the time, the Democrats often argued among themselves and lacked a strong issue that could unite them. Douglas hoped that westward settlement and popular sovereignty would bring the Democrats together. Their major opponents, the Whigs, generally opposed both issues.

President Franklin Pierce supported the Kansas-Nebraska Act and the repeal of the Missouri Compromise. With his support, Congress passed the law in a close vote. Douglas, however, had not realized how much the new law would anger some Northern Democrats. They did not want to expand slavery in the West, and some left the party because of the Kansas-Nebraska Act. The Whigs also split apart over the issue. Some of these former Democrats and Whigs, along with members of the Free-Soil Party, joined together to form a new, antislavery party, the Republicans.

Despite the use of this illustration in his 1856 presidential campaign showing his bravery John C. Frémont lost the election to James Buchanan.

THE BIRTH OF THE REPUBLICANS

The Kansas-Nebraska Act led Northerners from both major parties to meet and discuss forming a new party that would oppose the spread of slavery. Joining them were members of a third party, the Free-Soilers. On March 20, 1854, about fifty of these anti-Nebraska forces met at a small schoolhouse in Ripon, Wisconsin—a meeting often called the birth of the Republican Party. The party held its first convention a few months later in Michigan. The Republicans condemned the Kansas-Nebraska Act, because it would put "a thousand miles of slave soil...between the free states of the Atlantic and those of the Pacific." In 1856, John C. Frémont ran as the party's first presidential candidate. The Republican slogan for that year was "Free Soil, Free Labor, Free Speech, Free Men, Frémont."

"Bleeding Kansas"

In May 1854, Congress let the first American settlers enter Kansas. A Massachusetts mill owner named Eli Thayer organized some of these first arrivals. He opposed the abolitionist movement (the movement to abolish slavery), and he supported popular sovereignty. Some Northern settlers, however, openly favored Kansas's becoming a free state.

Other early settlers in Kansas came from neighboring Missouri. Some of these Missourians owned slaves and hoped that Kansas would become a slave state. Even those settlers from Missouri who did not own slaves opposed abolitionism and supported slavery in the territory. In 1855, the two groups of settlers—Missourians and Northerners—fought to gain control of Kansas's government.

In the first election in Kansas, Missourians who lived near the border illegally crossed into the territory to vote. This action angered Northern settlers in Kansas and Northern politicians in Washington, D.C. In 1855, during another election, armed Missourians crossed into Kansas. Once again, they voted illegally and threatened the officials who ran the polls. Senator David Rice Atchison of Missouri led this effort to influence the vote. He claimed that he could send 5,000 followers into Kansas—enough, he said, to "kill every...abolitionist in the Territory."

The tensions grew after the fall of 1855, when antislavery Kansans asked Congress to let Kansas enter the Union as a free state. They declared that the territorial government chosen by the proslavery forces was illegal. Fighting broke out between the two sides, with more Missourians crossing over the border to battle the slavery opponents. President Pierce called for an end to the fighting, though he supported the proslavery forces.

Fast Fact

The constitution drafted by the free-state Kansans outlawed slavery but banned free blacks from entering the territory.

Fast Fact

The Missourians who crossed into Kansas to vote and threaten people were called "Border Ruffians."

The fighting continued into 1856, as slavery supporters threatened the citizens of Lawrence, Kansas. In response, abolitionist John Brown led an attack that killed five proslavery Kansans. By now, the territory was known across the country as "Bleeding Kansas," and the troubles there continued until government troops arrived and restored order.

Famous Figures

JOHN BROWN
(1800–1859)

Born in Connecticut, John Brown settled in Ohio and became one of the most vocal abolitionists in the country. Unlike most opponents of slavery, Brown eventually advocated the use of violence to pursue his goals. A deeply religious man, he claimed that his actions served God's will. After he left Kansas, Brown tried to organize a slave rebellion. His first step was to steal weapons from the U.S. armory at Harpers Ferry, Virginia (now West Virginia). The effort failed, and Brown was arrested and hanged for committing treason. To slaves, Brown offered hope that more white Americans would actively support ending slavery. To Southerners, he represented the dangers of the abolitionist movement. Many Northerners supported his goals, if not his calls for violence.

In Defense of the Kansas-Nebraska Act

For years, Stephen Douglas had wanted to promote settlement in the West by creating a new territory. The Nebraska Territory, he argued, would link the Midwest with the Pacific. At the time, the land was filled with Native American tribes. Douglas said that the United States could not defend the West Coast or promote economic growth there until American settlers filled the Great Plains. Settlement, he said, was the only way to "develop, cherish, and protect our immense interests and possessions on the Pacific." Settlement would also help railroad investors in his state, who wanted to build a new railway that would cross this region.

Popular sovereignty was the key to winning Southern support for Douglas's plan. Some Southern lawmakers hoped that a new railroad would take a southerly route, instead of starting in Chicago, Illinois, and cutting through Nebraska and other Northern territories. By promoting popular sovereignty in Kansas and Nebraska, Douglas hoped to win Southern support for his railroad plan.

Popular sovereignty was similar to the notion of states' rights, which the Southern states had favored for decades. In general, the slave states did not want the national government limiting the states' actions—especially regarding slavery. Southerners wanted territories to have every chance possible to allow slavery. They feared that if the country had more free states than slave states, the free states would elect representatives and senators who would try to end slavery.

Letting the people in the territories decide would also take the slavery issue out of Congress, where it had caused much bad feeling. One Whig newspaper said that passing the Kansas-Nebraska Act would "promote the peace of the country, the restoration of good feeling between the North and the South, and the consequent strength and perpetuity of our glorious Union."

> *Fast Fact*
>
> Despite the presence of Southern slave owners in Kansas, the territory entered the Union as a free state in 1861, just before the start of the Civil War (1861–1865).

Other supporters of the Kansas-Nebraska Act argued that the Missouri Compromise was unconstitutional and that Congress never had the legal right to set limits on slavery within a state. Even if that law had been legal, the Compromise of 1850 had set up new rules. Under that law, slavery could be allowed above the Missouri Compromise line, if voters in Utah or New Mexico chose to have it. Citizens in other new territories above that latitude should have the same right.

In Their Own Words

Here is part of an editorial published by the *Detroit Free Press*, a Democratic newspaper, supporting the Kansas-Nebraska Act.

Nothing can be clearer than that the national democratic party, at the close of the slavery excitement in 1850, settled down upon the doctrines...that Congress possesses no power over the subject of slavery in the States or Territories, and that any legislation in that behalf is unconstitutional and void. The compromise measures adopted in 1850 were based upon this doctrine.

In Opposition to the Kansas-Nebraska Act

Douglas's opponents in Congress and across the North believed that Kansas and Nebraska should not have popular sovereignty. The Missouri Compromise had clearly stated that slavery was illegal north of 36 degrees, 30 minutes. The decision made in the Compromise of 1850 regarding popular sovereignty did not apply in this case. Utah and New Mexico were not part of the Louisiana Purchase; Kansas and Nebraska were. Trying to overturn the Missouri Compromise, one Whig newspaper said, was a "gigantic...crime."

Critics of the Kansas-Nebraska Act feared that if new western states chose to allow slavery, the slave states would dominate Congress. Then Southern lawmakers could stop any future attempts to limit slavery. Some Northern Whigs referred to a "slave power conspiracy" that was trying to force the Kansas-Nebraska Act through Congress.

Northerners had many reasons for opposing the spread of slavery. Some believed that it was against Christian teachings. Others hoped that immigrants would settle in the Nebraska and Kansas Territories. They might be less likely to move there if slavery were established, since the slaves would do jobs that immigrants might otherwise be hired to do. The presence of slaves would also tend to keep wages low and make employers less likely to improve conditions for free workers. Said Senator Salmon Chase of New York, "Labor cannot be respected where any class of laborers is held in...bondage."

Illinois senator Stephen A. Douglas was the creator of the 1854 Kansas-Nebraska Act. One of his goals was to relieve tensions over slavery. Douglas is pictured here around the time of the 1860 presidential campaign, in which he ran against, and was defeated by, Abraham Lincoln.

Douglas had hoped that the Kansas-Nebraska Act would solve some of the country's divisions over slavery. Instead, the law led to stronger negative feelings between the two sides. As one U.S. politician later noted, the Kansas-Nebraska Act "produced a frenzy of [anger] on the part of thousands and tens of thousands in both old parties who had never before taken any part whatsoever in antislavery agitation."

In Their Own Words

Here is part of a statement written by Salmon Chase against the Kansas-Nebraska Act.

[Some] may tell you that the Union can be maintained only by submitting to the demands of slavery. We tell you that the safety of the Union can only be insured by the full recognition of the just claims of freedom and man....

Whatever apologies may be offered for the toleration of slavery in the states, none can be urged for its extension into territories where it does not exist and where that extension involves the repeal of ancient law.

CHAPTER EIGHT

The Dred Scott Case

WHAT
Dred Scott, an African American slave,
goes to court to seek his freedom.

ISSUES
The citizenship of African Americans and the power of Congress
to forbid slavery in U.S. territories

WHERE
Missouri

WHEN
1857

*D*uring the first half of the nineteenth century, some Southern slaves won their freedom through the U.S. courts. At times, slave owners brought their slaves with them when they moved into territories or states that did not allow slavery. When they returned to a slave state, some slaves argued that they had technically won their freedom, since they had lived in a free region for a period. At first, Northern courts rejected the idea that slaves won their freedom if their masters traveled into free states for a long period but did not actually own homes there. By the 1830s, however, some courts said that slaves did earn their freedom if their masters took them to free states, even without actually setting up residences there.

In 1846, two slaves, Dred Scott and his wife Harriet, sued their owner, Irene Emerson, to try to win their freedom. They probably received support from the Blows, Dred Scott's former owners, and some white lawyers who helped them by charging small or no fees. Irene Emerson had acquired the slaves from her husband, Dr. John Emerson. The Emersons lived in St. Louis, Missouri, where slavery was allowed. During the 1830s, however, Dr. Emerson had taken Dred Scott with him when he served as a military doctor in Illinois, a free state, and Wisconsin, a territory that did not allow slavery. (Scott married his wife during this period. At the time, slaves could not marry in slave states.) Now, back in Missouri, the Scotts claimed that they should be given their freedom.

In the past, several Missouri courts had ruled in favor of slaves who had returned to the state after living with their masters in free states or territories. In this case, however, the court ruled against the Scotts on a technical issue: Irene Emerson's lawyer questioned whether or not she actually was their owner during their most recent stay in Missouri. If she was

Fast Fact

Even if slaves won their freedom in the North, they did not have the same legal rights as whites. Most could not vote, and two Northern states, Indiana and Illinois, did not allow free blacks within their borders.

not, then the Scotts could not sue her. The jury ruled that the Scotts' lawyer had not proven that Emerson was their owner and denied their claim for freedom.

Famous Figures

DRED SCOTT
(?–1858)

Historians have some questions about the early life of Dred Scott. Scott was most likely born between 1790 and 1810, probably in Virginia. His first owner was a Virginian named Peter Blow. In 1830, Blow and his family settled in St. Louis. Sometime before 1833, the Blows sold Scott to John Emerson.

Scott married his wife, Harriet, around 1837. They had two daughters, Eliza and Lizzie. Scott remained a slave until May 1857. That year, Irene Emerson and her new husband, Calvin Chaffee, gave their rights to Scott to Taylor Blow, the son of Scott's first owner. Scott had a good relationship with Blow's children, and Taylor Blow freed the entire Scott family.

The Court Battles Continue

With the help of white lawyers, Scott continued to sue for his freedom. (Although the case involved separate trials for Scott and his wife, most historians focus just on Dred's case.

The legal issues were the same in both cases.) Scott appealed his case to the Missouri Supreme Court, still claiming that Irene Emerson was his legal owner at the time that he filed his suit. His lawyers wanted a new trial in the state circuit court, arguing that the law was on Scott's side and that a small technical point should not prevent him from winning his freedom. In June 1848, the Supreme Court agreed, and Scott's second trial began in 1850.

This time Scott won his case, but Irene Emerson's lawyers made their own appeal to the state's Supreme Court. They argued that John Emerson's trips to Illinois and Wisconsin were part of his military duty—he did not choose to go to a free state or territory. In that case, the lawyers said, the old legal rulings regarding taking a slave into free lands should not apply. By this time, Irene Emerson's brother, John Sanford, was Scott's owner and was pursuing the case to keep him as a slave.

Since 1848, slavery had been a widely divisive issue in the United States. In the North, more people wanted to limit the spread of slavery or abolish it altogether. In slave states, such as Missouri, whites who supported slavery felt that their values and their freedom were coming under attack. By 1852, the judges on the Missouri Supreme Court were more supportive of slavery than the previous judges had been. They overturned the lower court's ruling that set Scott free.

The judges wrote that one state did not have to accept the laws of another. The fact that slavery was illegal in Illinois had no effect on Missouri and its right to allow slavery. The judges also chose to ignore that, in the past, Missouri

Fast Fact

Dred Scott's first trial was held in a circuit court. In the eighteenth and nineteenth centuries, judges in these courts heard cases in several locations within a district—the judges were said to ride a circuit. A circuit court is often called a lower court. A case decided in a lower court can be appealed to a court with more authority, such as a supreme court.

courts had accepted the idea that a slave, once free in another state or territory, was always free. The judges noted that opinions on slavery had changed in recent years and that antislavery forces had gained power in the country. The judges did not want to give in to those forces, which they felt were "possessed with a dark...spirit in relation to slavery" and sought "the overthrow and destruction of our government."

Legal Issues

Scott's next step was to take his case to a federal circuit court. He wanted the U.S. government to step in and overturn the Missouri Supreme Court's decision. The new trial introduced a new element: whether African Americans were citizens of a state or the country. Sanford's lawyer said that Scott was not a citizen and had no legal grounds for taking the case to a federal court. The circuit court judge disagreed and let the case continue. The trial also raised the issue of whether Congress had the right to outlaw slavery in territories. Congress had done so with the Missouri Compromise.

With that law, passed in 1820, Congress limited slavery in parts of the lands that had formed the Louisiana Purchase, a large area west of the Mississippi River. The United States had bought Louisiana from France in 1803. Missouri, a new state carved out of the territory, was allowed to enter the Union as a slave state. At the same time, Maine joined as a free state. As part of the Missouri Compromise, Congress drew an imaginary line west from the southern border of Missouri. The line followed a line of northern latitude that measured 36 degrees, 30 minutes. Above the line, slavery would be outlawed; below it, a territory had the right to allow slavery. Wisconsin, the territory where Dred Scott had lived with Dr. Emerson, was above that line.

ANOTHER IMPORTANT CASE

In 1851, the U.S. Supreme Court decided another case that related to slavery. In *Strader v. Graham,* the court said that each state could decide the status of the people living within its borders, using its own laws. For slaves, this meant that going to a free state and then returning to a slave state did not change their status as slaves. The thinking in *Strader* influenced the final decision in the Dred Scott case.

On to the Supreme Court

In the federal court, the judge ruled that the laws of Missouri applied, not the laws of Illinois. Scott was still a slave. Scott had just one hope left: taking his case to the U.S. Supreme Court. The case was filed in 1854, but the court did not hear it until 1856. Finally, on March 6, 1857, the court gave its decision. Chief Justice Roger Taney said that Scott was not a citizen and therefore did not have a right to sue in federal court at all. The issue was not whether Scott was free or a slave—African Americans could not be citizens. In addition, slaves were property, and slave owners had legal protections to stop the state or other people from illegally taking their property from them.

With that decision, Taney asserted that the Supreme Court had no right to decide the case, since Scott never had the right to bring it. Still, the judges offered their opinion on the other legal issues raised in the case, including whether Scott's stay in a free state—Illinois—meant that he was free in a slave state, too. Based on the earlier decision the court had made in *Strader v. Graham,* the justices now stated that the Illinois law outlawing slavery had no effect on Scott once he returned to Missouri.

Famous Figures

ROGER TANEY
(1777–1864)

Legal scholars consider Roger Taney to be one of the greatest chief justices of the U.S. Supreme Court. Some of his decisions helped give more Americans new economic opportunities, and he tried to balance the interests of the states and the federal government. Today, however, he is best known for his decision in the Dred Scott case—and often criticized for it.

Taney grew up on a tobacco plantation in Maryland, a slave state. After studying law, he entered politics. In 1831, he was named attorney general for the United States. Five years later, he took over as chief justice of the Supreme Court. In the Scott case, Taney showed his sympathy for the interests of Southern slave owners. He shared the racist views that many whites—including some who opposed slavery—had about African Americans. On his own plantation, however, Taney had freed his slaves more than thirty years before he made his historic legal decision.

Praise for the Scott Decision

Proslavery forces welcomed the Supreme Court's decision. Slave owners and their supporters felt that they were under increasing attack from antislavery lawmakers and abolitionists, those who wanted to abolish slavery. The Dred Scott case seemed to boost their chances of keeping blacks in slavery. Taney stated that neither the Declaration of Independence nor the Constitution applied to African Americans. When those documents were written, he said, all Europeans saw blacks as "beings of an...order...so far inferior that they had no rights which the white man was bound to respect."

Newspapers and lawmakers in slave states believed that with the ruling, the country would finally stop arguing over slavery. The risk of disunion, or the country's splitting into separate nations, was now lowered. Some speakers also praised Taney for his legal wisdom and courage.

President James Buchanan also supported the decision. Elected in 1856, he became president just a few days before the Supreme Court made its ruling. Buchanan hoped that the court's ruling in the Dred Scott case would settle the slavery issue for good. Several years after the decision, the president said that the ruling had assured "the prosperity of the Territories, as well as the tranquility of the States."

In Their Own Words

Here is part of an article from a Charleston, South Carolina, newspaper on the Dred Scott decision.

The Supreme Court of the United States, in a recent case, has...established as law what our Southern statesmen have been repeating daily for many years on the floors of Congress, that the whole action of this Government on the subject of slavery, for more than a quarter of a century...has been all beyond the limits of the Constitution; was without justifiable authority; and that the whole mass should be now proclaimed null and void, and that slavery is guaranteed by the constitutional compact.

Anger over the Dred Scott Decision

The arguments against the Dred Scott decision began in the Supreme Court itself. Two justices, John McLean and Benjamin Curtis, wrote separate dissenting opinions. They both argued that the Supreme Court did have the legal right to hear the case. Then they noted that many previous courts had ruled in favor of slaves seeking their freedom after being taken to free states. McLean also said that in addressing this and other issues, Taney had talked about legal points not related to the Scott case. Those arguments, McLean and others believed, were personal opinions and should not have influenced the court's decision.

Outside the Supreme Court, abolitionists and other Americans reacted strongly against the decision. Many belonged to the Republican Party, which had formed in 1854 to oppose the spread of slavery. Some noted that most of the judges who ruled against Scott were Southerners who owned or once owned slaves. The antislavery forces believed that the judges had acted on their personal beliefs, not on the law.

Antislavery forces attacked the notion that the Constitution and the Declaration of Independence denied African Americans their legal rights. Others said that Congress did have a right to set laws for the territories, which it had been doing for seventy years.

Not surprisingly, some of the strongest comments came from free blacks. With the Dred Scott decision, the Supreme Court had taken away any legal rights that they had enjoyed in the past. At a meeting in Philadelphia, Pennsylvania, free blacks asserted that in the future they would "denounce" the Constitution because now, in the eyes of the U.S. legal system, free blacks were "inferior and degraded beings."

Fast Fact

Obiter dictum is the legal term for a judicial decision based on ideas not directly related to a case. The Latin term means "said in passing." Historians still debate if Taney's decision was shaped by *obiter dictum*.

Unlike President Buchanan and some Southerners, the opponents of the Dred Scott decision did not believe that the slavery issue had been settled for good. The decision, along with other slavery-related issues of the 1850s, drove the country toward the Civil War (1861–1865).

In Their Own Words

In 1857, Abraham Lincoln supported the views of Justices McLean and Curtis on the Dred Scott decision. He also attacked the idea that the Declaration of Independence did not apply to African Americans. Here is part of what he said.

I think the authors of [the Declaration] intended to include all men, but they did not intend to declare all men equal in all respects. They did not mean to say all were equal in color, size, intellect, moral developments or social capacity. They defined…in what respects they did consider all men created equal—equal with "certain inalienable rights, among which are life, liberty and the pursuit of happiness." This they said, and this they meant.

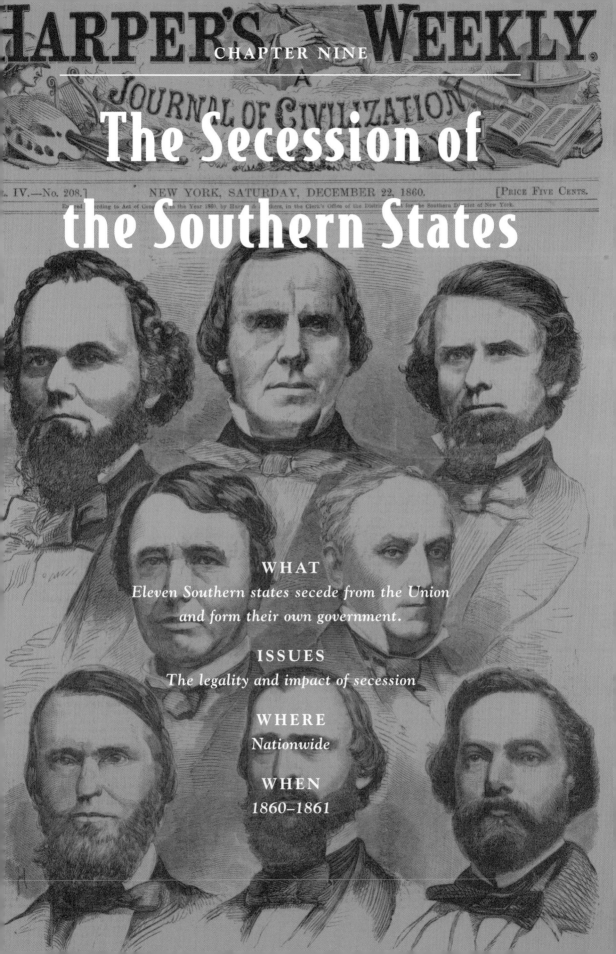

HARPER'S WEEKLY.

A JOURNAL OF CIVILIZATION.

. IV.—No. 208.]   NEW YORK, SATURDAY, DECEMBER 22, 1860.   [PRICE FIVE CENTS.

Entered according to Act of Congress, in the Year 1860, by Harper & Brothers, in the Clerk's Office of the District Court for the Southern District of New York.

CHAPTER NINE

The Secession of the Southern States

WHAT

Eleven Southern states secede from the Union
and form their own government.

ISSUES

The legality and impact of secession

WHERE

Nationwide

WHEN

1860–1861

Throughout the first half of the nineteenth century, political leaders in various states considered secession, or breaking off from the Union, for various reasons. During the War of 1812 (1812-1815), some New Englanders who did not support the war or the ruling Democratic-Republican Party hinted that New England should secede. South Carolina considered secession in 1832 in order to assert its right to overturn a tax law that it did not like. One issue, however, threatened to break up the Union more than any other: slavery. At times, both antislavery forces in the North and proslavery forces in the South considered secession the only answer to settling the two regions' differences over slavery.

This engraving, which dates from 1822, shows two white men harassing a free black man. The end of slavery in the North by the early 1800s did not mean that blacks there had any rights, and in the South, slavery had grown steadily.

At the founding of the United States in 1776, all thirteen states allowed slavery. The Constitution, written in 1787, did not place any limits on slavery. (It did, however, give a time limit of twenty years for bringing new slaves into the country.) By then, however, some Northern states were already ending slavery or planning for its gradual end in the future. At the same time, the Southern states were committed to slavery, since their economy relied on the work that slaves performed. The use of slaves grew during the early nineteenth century as more Southern farmers began raising cotton. The crop grew best in warm, humid climates, and raising it was hard work.

During the 1840s, U.S. lawmakers frequently debated allowing slavery in new states and territories. Many Northern politicians wanted to halt the spread of slavery if they could not end it altogether. Southerners felt that if slavery was not allowed in more states and territories, Congress would eventually be controlled by antislavery forces that would end slavery altogether.

AMERICA'S SLAVE POPULATION

In 1790, the United States had just under 700,000 slaves. Every state had some slaves, but more than 600,000 of them lived in just four Southern states: Virginia, Maryland, North Carolina, and South Carolina. By 1860, the country had almost 4 million slaves—all but a handful in Southern states. That year, the states with the largest slave populations were Virginia, Georgia, Mississippi, and Alabama.

A Bitter Election

For many years, Democrats from all parts of the country tended to support slavery—or at least a state's right to choose whether or not to allow it. In the 1860 presidential election, however, the Democrats split along regional lines over slavery. Northern Democrats supported Illinois senator Stephen Douglas, who called for popular sovereignty—the voters in each territory should decide if they would allow slavery. Southern Democrats, however, were strongly proslavery, and to them, popular sovereignty did not do enough to guarantee that new slave states would enter the Union. The Southern Democrats chose their own presidential candidate, John Breckinridge, the U.S. vice president at the time.

During the 1850s, members of different parties who opposed slavery had formed a new party, the Republicans. In 1860, they chose Abraham Lincoln as their candidate. Lincoln was sure to win the votes of most antislavery people. The Republicans also argued that the Democrats had run the country poorly during the past eight years. Lincoln and his supporters promised to strengthen the economy and protect the rights of immigrants.

Democrats told voters that a vote for Lincoln was a vote for disunion, because some Southern states threatened to secede if the Republicans won. In some Southern states, lawmakers planned for secession even before the November election.

An 1860 political cartoon depicted that year's presidential election as a "Political Quadrille" with "Music by Dred Scott." (A quadrille is a type of dance, and Scott's presence represents the impact of his Supreme Court case on the election.) Abraham Lincoln is in the upper right corner.

A fourth party also ran a candidate that year. The Constitutional Union Party was centered in Kentucky, Virginia, and Tennessee. Most of its members were Southerners who hated the Democratic Party but wanted to preserve slavery. The party's goals were to keep the Union together and defend the Constitution. It chose John Bell of Tennessee as its candidate.

With proslavery forces split, no one party dominated the South. Breckinridge won the Deep South, while Bell took Virginia, Tennessee, and Kentucky. Douglas won only one state, Missouri, and split the vote in New Jersey with Lincoln. Across the North and in California and Oregon, Lincoln won easily, giving him the election.

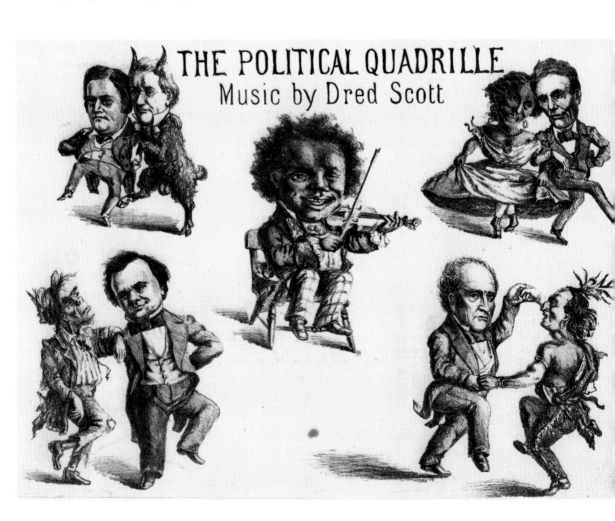

THE GEOGRAPHY OF THE SOUTH

Arkansas, Tennessee, Virginia, and North Carolina formed what is sometimes called the Upper South. Slave states farther south were sometimes called the Deep or Lower South. Kentucky, Missouri, Maryland, and Delaware were the so-called border states. These slave states formed a border between the free states to the North and the other slave-owning states.

A Search for Compromise

Lincoln's election stirred debate across the South, as politicians considered secession. South Carolina was the first to act. On December 20, 1860, its lawmakers said "that the union now subsisting between South Carolina and other states, under the name of 'The United States of America' is hereby dissolved." A few weeks later, six other states from the Deep South joined South Carolina.

While the Southern states were debating secession, some members of Congress from both the North and the South tried to find a way to keep the Union together. Kentucky senator John Crittenden suggested several amendments to the Constitution to address Southern concerns. Some Northerners, however, were not ready to compromise. They did not want to give in to the South, and some were prepared to fight to keep the Union together. One Pittsburgh newspaper editor noted that "the public mind is so inflamed against Compromise and so bitter against all efforts at concession.... It amounts almost to a fury."

Most Southerners in the states that had already seceded also rejected the idea of compromise. In early February 1861, representatives from the seven seceding states met in Montgomery, Alabama. They formed a new government based largely on the government

Fast Fact

The six states that seceded after South Carolina were Texas, Florida, Alabama, Mississippi, Louisiana, and Georgia. In April 1861, when the Civil War began, four more states joined them: North Carolina, Virginia, Arkansas, and Tennessee. The four border slave states remained in the Union.

created under the U.S. Constitution, though with a weaker Supreme Court. The states decided to call their new country the Confederate States of America, and soon they elected Jefferson Davis as their first president.

Famous Figures

JEFFERSON DAVIS
(1808–1889)

Before the Civil War (1861–1865), Jefferson Davis served in the U.S. military and then entered politics. Twice, he represented Mississippi in the U.S. Senate, and he served as secretary of war under President Franklin Pierce. A slave owner and one of the major political leaders in the South, Davis called for the expansion of slavery. After Lincoln's election, Davis supported secession. He hoped to receive a high post in the Confederate military, but instead accepted the presidency of the new Southern government. As president, Davis sometimes made bad decisions and argued with his generals and Confederate lawmakers. After the Civil War, Davis spent two years in jail for treason. For the rest of his life, he remained convinced that the South had taken the right step by seceding from the Union.

The Start of the Civil War

The Confederacy was determined to use its authority as quickly as possible. The new government took control of federal forts and armories within its borders. Lincoln would be sworn in as president on March 4, and the South was preparing for a possible war. Southerners thought that the Republican Party was determined to end slavery, later if not sooner. Lincoln's election, one Southerner wrote, was the "declaration of an unceasing war against slavery as an institution."

Lincoln, at his inauguration, discussed the crisis that the country faced. He said that he had "no purpose…to interfere with the institution of slavery in the States where it exists." The president also said that he believed the Union of the states was permanent—no state could legally secede. He was prepared to do whatever was necessary to keep the Union together.

Although the Confederacy had taken control of many federal forts, the Union still held Fort Sumter in Charleston, South Carolina. By April 1861, the fort was surrounded by Confederate troops. Lincoln made plans to send supplies to the Union troops at Fort Sumter, but on April 12, before the supplies arrived, the Confederacy attacked the fort. The next day, the Union commander surrendered the fort, and the Civil War had begun.

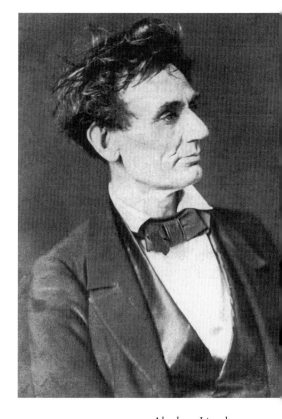

Abraham Lincoln, photographed in 1857. At the time he was practicing law, after having served one term as a U.S. representative from Illinois.

The Arguments for Secession

To slave owners and their Southern supporters, threatening secession was the only way to protect slavery in the United States. Republicans said that they only wanted to stop the spread of slavery, but too many Northerners had shown their support for ending it altogether. One Southern senator warned that the federal government would fill positions in the South with people who were for abolition—abolishing all slavery.

In the view of the South, even if the North did not take new steps to end slavery, the federal government and many Northerners had already pursued illegal actions. In its statement calling for secession, South Carolina claimed that the government had tried to take away Southerners' right to own property—slaves. The secessionists believed that the Northerners were ignoring the constitutional right to own property.

Many Southerners argued that secession would also bring new, positive benefits to the South. Forming the Confederacy, some Southerners argued, was just the first step toward creating a large, prosperous, slave-owning country. This new nation would stretch from the Atlantic Ocean to the Pacific Ocean and perhaps reach down into Mexico and the Caribbean, dominating trade in the region.

To some Southerners, preserving slavery through secession was a noble act. Slavery, they believed, was good for both the black slaves and their white owners. Daniel DeJarnette, a Virginia lawmaker, argued that "there is more...contentment and happiness, among the slaves of the South, than any laboring population on the globe." Slave owners also claimed that slavery was accepted in the Bible and that God wanted Christians to own slaves.

In Their Own Words

Here is part of the South Carolina declaration for secession.

On the 4th of March next [the Republican] Party will take possession of the government. It has announced that the South shall be excluded from the common territory...and that a war must be waged against slavery until it shall cease throughout the United States. The guarantees of our Constitution will then no longer exist; the equal rights of the states will be lost....
We, therefore, the people of South Carolina...have solemnly declared...that the state of South Carolina has resumed her position among the nations of the world, as [a] separate and independent state.

A CONCERN FOR MONEY

Some Northern business owners spoke out against secession. They feared the possible damage to their business dealings in the South. In New York City, the mayor suggested that the city itself should secede if the South did not rejoin the Union. That way, if the two sides fought a war, New York businesses could keep their ties with the South. New York City's lawmakers rejected the idea.

Fighting Secession

After Lincoln's election, many Northerners and some Southern lawmakers argued that the country had to stay together. Lincoln thought that secession was illegal. James Buchanan, who served as president before Lincoln, thought that a state could secede if the government took illegal actions. However, Lincoln had been legally elected and hadn't done anything illegal as president, since he hadn't taken over yet. Buchanan said that the Southern concern for any "future dangers" that Lincoln might commit "is no good reason for an immediate dissolution of the Union."

In the South, some lawmakers who opposed secession were willing to wait and see what Lincoln did about slavery before taking any action. Lincoln was limited in what he could do anyway, since Congress shaped the country's laws. Despite Lincoln's election, the Democrats still controlled both the House of Representatives and the Senate. They could stop most Republican efforts to hurt the South.

As the attempts at compromise showed, some Northerners were willing to give slavery legal protection. At a February 1861 meeting called by Virginia, Northern representatives supported an amendment to the Constitution that would prevent Congress from ever passing a law abolishing slavery. In several Northern cities, thousands of citizens signed petitions supporting the compromise efforts.

Other Americans opposed secession because they feared civil war. Pro-Union forces knew that the federal government would have to fight to preserve the Union if secession continued. Stephen Douglas was one Northern senator who spoke against secession. He said, "Better that all political organizations be broken up...than that the Union be destroyed and the country plunged into civil war."

The arguments against secession, however, did not keep the Union together. Just as many people predicted, the issue between the North and South had to be settled with a long and bloody civil war.

In Their Own Words

Through February 1861, Senator John Crittenden of Kentucky tried to work out a deal in Congress that would keep the seceding states in the Union. When his compromise plan failed, he delivered a speech in the Senate. Here is part of what he said.

Hold fast to the Union. There is safety, tried safety, known safety.... We are one people in blood; in language one; in thoughts one.... If...we wish to carry with us grateful hearts of the blessings we have enjoyed, we shall be bound to compromise with the difficulties that must occur on all the ways of the world that are [followed] by governments on earth. It is our [fate] to have such difficulties. Let it be our...wisdom to compromise and settle them.

CHAPTER TEN

The Freeing of the Slaves

WHAT

President Abraham Lincoln frees the slaves in the Confederate states with the Emancipation Proclamation; the Thirteenth Amendment frees all American slaves.

ISSUES

The benefits and dangers of freeing the slaves

WHERE

Nationwide

WHEN

1863 and 1865

*I*n late 1860 and early 1861, eleven Southern states seceded, or broke away from the United States. The states then formed their own country, the Confederate States of America. Many Confederate citizens made clear that slavery was a key issue behind their actions. These Southerners believed that the North wanted to abolish slavery, after fighting to prevent its spread in western territories. When it left the Union, Mississippi argued that the Constitution allowed slavery and that "all efforts to impair its value or lessen its duration...is a violation of the compact of the Union."

In the North, the efforts to end slavery were led by the abolitionists. Since the 1830s, these whites and free blacks had argued that slavery was wrong and should be abolished immediately. More moderate Northerners knew that the thought of abolition angered Southerners and could lead to a civil war. The moderates called for limiting the spread of slavery, not ending it. By 1860, however, more Northerners were starting to accept the idea that slavery should not exist anywhere in the United States.

Fast Fact

In 1863, the north-western region of Virginia, which had remained loyal to the Union, became the separate state of West Virginia.

Abraham Lincoln, elected president in November 1860, was not an abolitionist. On a personal level, he thought that slavery was wrong. He believed that the men who drafted the U.S. Constitution in 1787 expected slavery to end at some future date. As a politician, however, Lincoln realized that the Southern states did have a legal right to allow slavery. The federal government, he said during an 1860 speech, did not have the power to emancipate, or free, Southern slaves. When the Southern states seceded and formed the Confederacy, Lincoln did not want to fight to end slavery. He fought the Civil War (1861–1865) to keep the Union together.

MIXED MESSAGES
ABOUT AFRICAN AMERICANS

After his death, Abraham Lincoln was often praised for his efforts to free the slaves. During his political career, however, he denied that African Americans and whites should have the same legal rights. In 1858, he said, "I have no purpose to introduce political and social equality between the white and black races." Since they could not be equal, whites should have "the superior position." Lincoln also favored sending free African Americans to their own colony in Central America or the West Indies, islands in the Caribbean Sea. As president, he tried to do this during the Civil War. Yet Lincoln also said that he believed that the Declaration of Independence included blacks in its claim that "all men are created equal." Also, he sincerely believed that slavery was wrong and that its existence threatened to damage the Union.

The Move toward Emancipation

Once the Civil War began, Lincoln tried to focus on the issue of preserving the Union. The war, he said, was a rebellion against the legal government of the United States. The question of freeing the slaves, however, was unavoidable. Abolitionists saw the war as a way to reach their goal. One African American abolitionist, Frederick Douglass, called for freeing the slaves and recruiting them into the Union army. Eventually, the North would use a large number of black troops, both slaves and free.

As the war went on, Congress took small steps to give slaves their freedom. It passed a law freeing any slaves who were forced to help the Confederacy's military efforts. The lawmakers also ordered Union military forces to protect slaves who ran away from their masters, instead of giving them back. Congress freed the slaves in Washington, D.C., and in the western territories as well.

Fast Fact

Three-quarters of the states had to approve the Thirteenth Amendment for it to become part of the Constitution. At the time, the country had thirty-six states, so twenty-seven votes were needed to ratify it. The current number of states required to approve an amendment is thirty-eight.

In 1862, Lincoln supported a law that would give money to states that gradually emancipated their slaves. By the end of the year, he decided to emancipate the slaves in Confederate states. His "Emancipation Proclamation," however, did not apply to all U.S. slaves. Four slave-owning states had remained loyal to the Union. Slaves in those states did not receive their freedom. Lincoln feared that freeing these slaves would push the four states to secede and join the Confederacy. The proclamation also did not apply in areas of some Confederate states, such as Virginia, that were pro-Union.

Lincoln declared that the Southern slaves were free, but while the war went on, slavery still existed in most of the Confederacy. By January 1865, however, several Confederate state governments had come under Union control. Slavery ended in Arkansas, Louisiana, and Tennessee. Two of the loyal slave states, Missouri and Maryland, ended slavery on their own. Congress also acted to guarantee that slavery would end everywhere in the United States. The lawmakers passed the Thirteenth Amendment to the Constitution, abolishing slavery. By the end of 1865, the amendment became law, after winning the approval of most of the states that had remained in the Union.

THE NEW PRESIDENT AND SLAVERY

By the time that the Thirteenth Amendment was passed, Andrew Johnson was the U.S. president. Lincoln had been assassinated on April 14, 1865 just days after the Civil War ended. Johnson, a slave owner, had been the military governor of Tennessee for part of the war. He had convinced Lincoln to let slavery continue in that state, which had seceded, but had come under Union control. Johnson eventually changed his mind and favored emancipation in Tennessee and across the country.

For and against the Emancipation Proclamation

During 1862, Lincoln came to accept the idea of emancipation—at least in the areas under Confederate control. At one time, he and other moderate Northerners worried that if slavery were abolished, the Southern states would never rejoin the Union. Since saving the Union was his first goal, Lincoln did not push for emancipation. As the war went on, however, he saw benefits to limited emancipation. "The moment came," he said, "when I felt that slavery must die that the nation might live." Lincoln realized that emancipation gave the Union military effort a higher purpose. The war was no longer merely about the political issue of keeping the Union together. Now, the war was also about ending a terrible wrong. Freeing the slaves also drew support from people overseas who supported the abolition of slavery, particularly the British.

Lincoln knew that he would win more political support from antislavery forces in the North who wanted him to take bold steps against slavery. They had criticized him for not attacking slavery from the beginning. He hoped that emancipation would shorten the war and limit the killing on both sides. He also hoped that Southern slaves, knowing that their freedom was at stake, would take a more active role in opposing their masters and helping the North. Emancipation also stirred the patriotism of free Northern blacks. Under the proclamation, they were allowed to serve in the military in large numbers. Many responded to this chance as a way to help end slavery for other African Americans.

At first President Lincoln was hesitant to free the slaves because he feared that such an act would make the Southern states even more intent on dissolving the Union. He eventually recognized, however, that emancipation would give the Union troops a higher purpose beyond the political aim of keeping the country together.

Fast Fact

In Mississippi, slaves formed a group called Lincoln's Legal Loyal League to spread the word about emancipation to other slaves across the state.

In the South, most people reacted harshly to the Emancipation Proclamation. One Southern paper said that "the devil triumphed" when Lincoln decided to free the slaves. A large number of Northerners also attacked the proclamation. Many of them belonged to the Democratic Party. They had fought against Lincoln, a Republican, when he ran for office in 1860. They also opposed the Civil War. Some Northern Democrats accepted slavery in the states where it already existed, even if they did not want it to spread. They considered the abolitionists to be political enemies who had tried to weaken the government with their calls for emancipation, both before the Civil War and since. One Democratic newspaper in Pennsylvania criticized Lincoln for listening to the "mad counsels and revolutionary teachings of the radical men of his party."

Some Northerners opposed freeing the slaves for more practical reasons. Under the Constitution, they argued, the president did not have the power to end slavery on his own, without any action by Congress. The proclamation, others said, would lengthen the war, not shorten it. The South would fight harder than ever, since it knew that slavery was at stake, and it would not seek to reenter the Union as long as its slaves were free. Pro-Union citizens in the Confederate states might also turn against the Union. They had argued that the Confederate states should rejoin the Union since Lincoln did not want to abolish slavery. The Emancipation Proclamation ended that argument for good.

Some Northerners also feared that white workers would now lose jobs to freed African Americans who came north looking for work. An Illinois newspaper wrote, "Our people are in great danger of being overrun by negroes set free by…the President's proclamation."

Not all of Lincoln's critics, however, were Democrats. Some Republicans thought that the Emancipation Proclamation would weaken support for the Union in the slave states that had not joined the Confederacy. Others thought that the president had not gone far enough and should have extended emancipation to all slaves. Lincoln remained convinced, however, that his moderate path was the best for the nation at that time.

In Their Own Words

On December 1, 1862, Lincoln spoke to Congress. He had already decided to free the Southern slaves, though he did not issue the Emancipation Proclamation until January 1, 1863. Here is part of Lincoln's 1862 speech on emancipation.

Without slavery, the rebellion could never have existed; without slavery it could not continue.... The proposed emancipation would shorten the war, perpetuate peace, insure the increase of population...and the wealth of the country.... In giving freedom to the slave, we assure the freedom of the free.

In Their Own Words

Here is part of an editorial from the *Valley Spirit,* a Democratic newspaper in Pennsylvania, criticizing Lincoln and his plan for emancipation.

But there is another aspect in which this subject is all important, that of its bearing upon the loyal Union men of the slave States.... They persistently denied the allegations of the Secessionists that this was war on the part of the Government for the abolition of Slavery.... President Lincoln, with one stroke of the pen...says to the whole southern people, that the Union men were wrong and the Secessionists were right.

This illustration is of the scene at the House of Representatives on January 31, 1865, the day the Thirteenth Amendment to the Constitution, which abolished slavery, was approved by the House.

The Debate over the Thirteenth Amendment

In 1864, President Lincoln supported an amendment to the Constitution abolishing slavery. Like some of his critics, he wondered if the Emancipation Proclamation was constitutional. Changing the Constitution itself to outlaw slavery would settle the question and extend emancipation to the entire Union. Once Southern states rejoined the Union, slave owners and Northern Democrats would not be able to use Congress to pass laws that allowed slavery in any form. The amendment would remove forever the issue that had led to war in the first place.

In Congress, some radical antislavery lawmakers wanted to do more than end slavery. They wanted the proposed Thirteenth Amendment to also protect the legal rights of the freed slaves. Massachusetts senator William Sumner led this effort. Other senators, however, disliked him personally and disliked his views on racial equality.

Supporters of the effort to end slavery feared that Sumner's opponents would defeat the abolition amendment if it were too closely associated with him. The amendment that passed in the Senate did not contain the wording that Sumner wanted.

The Senate passed the Thirteenth Amendment in 1864. One senator noted that the amendment would "restore to a whole race that freedom which is theirs by the gift of God." Republicans in Congress also saw the amendment as a political issue. In some areas of the country, voters welcomed abolition. Lawmakers from these areas wanted to be on record as opposing slavery, since they faced reelection campaigns in the fall.

Most Democrats opposed the amendment, and in the House, they were able to reject it the first time that it came up for a vote. Democrats feared that abolishing slavery would make it impossible for the North and South to ever have good relations. Some Democrats also based their opposition on racial grounds. If slaves received freedom, next they would receive the vote and other political rights. The opponents did not want to see this legal equality, because they believed that whites were superior to blacks. The government, one Democrat argued, "was made by white men and for white men." Giving slaves their freedom, a few Democrats added, would create public disorder, with angry whites who opposed abolition clashing with freed blacks.

Some Democrats said that the amendment was meant to destroy their party, not help African Americans. The Democrats were closely tied to proslavery forces. By ending slavery, the Republicans would take away the key issue that the Democrats had used to rally support. By January 1865, however, most Democrats realized that Northern voters wanted to end slavery. The politicians stood to lose future support—at least in the North—if they blocked the amendment. Many Democrats, even from slaveholding states, finally saw that slavery had to end for

Fast Fact

In 1839, former president John Quincy Adams had proposed a constitutional amendment to abolish slavery, but nothing came of it. The idea died until the vote of 1864.

the country to move forward. The House approved the amendment, and the states then began to ratify, or approve, it.

By the end of the year, most of the former slave states had also approved the Thirteenth Amendment. Approving the amendment was one of the conditions that Johnson had placed on the states to rejoin the Union. The Thirteenth Amendment was officially added to the Constitution in December 1865.

In Their Own Words

On February 1, 1865, President Lincoln thanked Congress for approving the Thirteenth Amendment. Here is part of a report on what he said.

He wished the reunion of all the States perfected and so effected as to remove all causes of disturbances in the future; and to attain this end it was necessary that the original disturbing cause should, if possible, be rooted out.... This amendment is a King's cure for all the evils. It winds the whole thing up.

In Their Own Words

In 1864, the *Valley Spirit* of Pennsylvania ran an editorial that was originally printed in the *Patriot and Union* newspaper. Here is part of that article, which attacked the Republicans and their reasons for passing the Thirteenth Amendment.

Let every Democrat in the land keep this fact steadily in view: That the Shoddy leaders care nothing for the abolition of slavery as a measure of philanthropy, but everything for it as a political measure. All their fine blather about "universal freedom"...is but the thin varnish over a magnificent political scheme by which they hope to destroy the Democratic party, and retain control of the...Government.

CHAPTER ELEVEN

Civil Rights for African Americans

WHAT
Congress proposes the Fourteenth and Fifteenth Amendments to
the Constitution, regarding civil rights for African Americans.

ISSUE
Equal legal rights for African Americans,
especially the right to vote

WHERE
Nationwide

WHEN
1866–1869

*E*ven before the Civil War (1861–1865) ended, President Abraham Lincoln made plans for how to bring the defeated South back into the Union. This "Reconstruction," however, was not completely worked out by the time that he was assassinated in April 1865. The new president, Andrew Johnson, along with Congress, would have to rebuild the South, which had been heavily damaged during the war. They also had to create new Southern state governments that were loyal to the Union and to settle the slavery issue once and for all.

By the end of 1865, the country had approved the Thirteenth Amendment, which abolished slavery. Congress then moved to protect the legal rights of the newly freed slaves, often called freedmen. The lawmakers sought new amendments that would protect freedmen and Northern blacks who were already free but often faced legal discrimination.

At this time, Congress was controlled by the Republican Party. Before the Civil War, the Republicans had opposed the spread of slavery into new territories. Some Republicans, however, had wanted a tougher position against slavery. They demanded its immediate abolition and equal treatment of blacks and whites. As Reconstruction began, these "Radical Republicans" won some influence in Congress. They shaped many of the policies affecting the newly freed slaves. Their leaders included William Sumner in the Senate and Thaddeus Stevens in the House of Representatives.

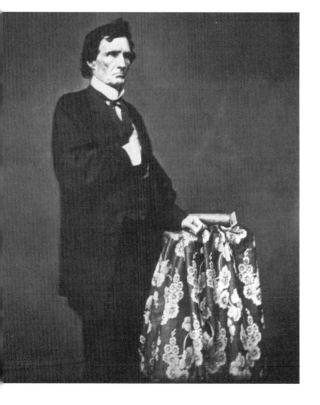

Thaddeus Stevens was a leader of the Radical Republicans in Congress. His views were considered radical because he was in favor of equal treatment for blacks and whites.

Moderate Republicans, however, outnumbered the Radicals, and they played a role in the Reconstruction process. The Radical Republicans also had to deal with President Johnson, a former slave owner who opposed many of their efforts.

Famous Figures

THADDEUS STEVENS
(1792–1868)

Born in Vermont, Thaddeus Stevens settled in Pennsylvania and first entered the House of Representatives in 1849. After losing his office in 1852, he returned to the House in 1859 and won his greatest fame after the Civil War. Known as a fine speaker and an honest politician, Stevens pushed for Radical Republican goals. He was one of America's strongest supporters of equal rights, though for a brief time, he opposed giving free blacks the right to vote. Stevens also wanted the U.S. government to give the farms of former Southern slave owners to the freedmen. Congress did not go along with this plan.

Protecting Civil Rights

Early in 1866, Congress proposed the Civil Rights Act. The law was meant to protect the civil rights of freedmen—such as their ability to enter contracts and receive equal treatment to whites in the workforce and the legal system. The Civil Rights Act was a reaction to new laws called "Black Codes" that some Southern states had passed to limit the rights of freedmen. One senator said that the act would "destroy all these discriminations" that the Southern states were trying to introduce.

President Johnson opposed the Civil Rights Act and vetoed it—he refused to sign it into law. Congress then used its constitutional right to pass the bill without the president's approval.

Johnson's veto of this bill and an earlier Reconstruction act angered many Republicans in Congress. To guarantee civil rights for African Americans, Congress proposed a constitutional amendment that would include many of the features of the Civil Rights Act.

THE BLACK CODES

After the Civil War, the U.S. government tried to limit the political power of former leaders of the Confederate States of America, the proslavery government that ruled the South during the war. Still, Southerners who had supported the old Confederacy and slavery did win political positions. In some states, the new leaders drafted "Black Codes"—laws that denied freedmen most of their legal rights. In November 1865, Mississippi was the first state to pass a Black Code. Under these laws, poor blacks under the age of eighteen were forced to serve as indentured servants. They had to work for whites—often their former slave masters—for a certain number of years. Supposedly, the arrangement was to give the freedmen training for jobs, but critics of the codes believed that Mississippi was trying to bring back a form of slavery. The state's Black Code also fined and jailed blacks who did not have jobs, and freedmen were not allowed to own guns or certain kinds of knives.

The Fourteenth and Fifteenth Amendments

The proposed amendment to protect civil rights was the Fourteenth Amendment. Congress passed it, even though Johnson strongly opposed it. The amendment said that all persons born in the United States were citizens of the country and of the state where they were born. Citizenship also applied to foreigners who went through a legal process to obtain it (naturalization). The Fourteenth Amendment also protected blacks—or any citizens—against state laws that tried to deny their civil rights.

The amendment limited the number of representatives that a state would have in Congress if it denied the right to vote to any male citizen. (Women at this time were still not allowed to vote.) This part of the amendment was meant to ensure that freed slaves could vote. Many Radical Republicans supported suffrage, or voting rights, for all African American men.

Congress also passed a law in 1867 designed to give Southern blacks the right to vote. The state governments had to approve black suffrage before they could reenter the Union. That law, however, was not a strong enough guarantee of voting rights. It also did not apply in Northern states or the former slave-owning states that had not joined the Confederacy. In 1869, Congress proposed a separate amendment, the Fifteenth, to guarantee black suffrage across the country.

At the same time that Congress was working for black civil rights, it limited some rights of former Confederates. One part of the Fourteenth Amendment dealt with Southerners who had held government positions before the war. If they had taken an oath to defend the U.S. Constitution and then supported the Confederacy, they could not hold government jobs in the future.

For an amendment to become part of the Constitution, three-quarters of the states must ratify, or approve, it. President Johnson had encouraged the Southern states not to ratify the Fourteenth Amendment. At the time, Congress was not letting elected representatives from the Southern states enter the Senate or the House. Johnson did not think that Congress should have passed the amendment without the Southern states represented. He also opposed any effort by Congress to get around his own plans for Reconstruction. Congress then passed a law saying that it

> *Fast Fact*
> The other early Reconstruction law that Johnson vetoed dealt with extending the operation of the Freedmen's Bureau. This government agency had been set up in March 1865 to help newly freed blacks. As with the Civil Rights Act, Congress passed the Freedmen's Bureau law despite Johnson's veto.

> *Fast Fact*
> Johnson was so opposed to the Fourteenth Amendment that he said he would spend $20,000 of his own money to try to prevent its ratification.

would accept the representatives from Southern states—if the states passed the amendment first. Later, Congress said that the Southern states must pass the Fourteenth Amendment to be accepted back into the Union. The amendment went into effect in 1868, and the Fifteenth Amendment was approved two years later.

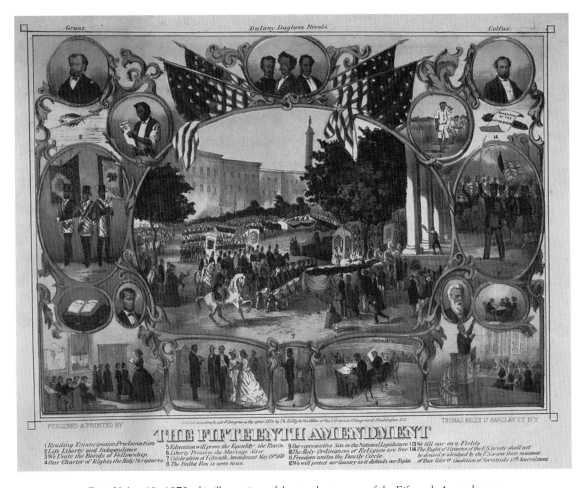

Dated May 19, 1870, this illustration celebrates the passage of the Fifteenth Amendment.

Republican Arguments for the Amendments

For more than 200 years, African American slaves had been treated as property, not humans. Then free blacks had been denied their rights. The Radical Republicans felt that they owed African Americans as much help as they could give them. Changing the Constitution was the only way to protect the legal rights of African Americans. The Republicans knew that their political foes might one day challenge federal laws that protected civil rights. The U.S. Supreme Court might rule against the laws, as it had earlier ruled in the 1859 Dred Scott case that African Americans were not U.S. citizens. If the Republicans passed an amendment, however, the courts would not be able to limit civil rights. Opponents of civil rights would have to pass their own amendment to overturn the Fourteenth and Fifteenth—a difficult legal process.

> *Fast Fact*
> In 1867, Congress passed separate laws giving African Americans in Washington, D.C., the right to vote and extending suffrage to all males in U.S. territories.

The Fourteenth Amendment was particularly important, because it prevented individual states from passing laws that violated the Bill of Rights or other amendments to the Constitution. Some of the Black Codes did limit these rights, such as an African American's right under the Second Amendment to own a gun. John A. Bingham, a moderate Republican, said that with the Fourteenth Amendment, "the powers of the States have been limited and the powers of Congress extended." Limiting the states' power, the Republicans believed, was the only way to guarantee equal rights for all Americans across the country.

The two amendments would also place limits on the power of the Southerners who had supported the Confederacy. Thaddeus Stevens noted that freedmen would form a large block of voters who would be loyal to the Union. Without black suffrage, he said, the Southern state governments "are sure to be ruled by traitors; and loyal men, black and white, will be oppressed, exiled, or murdered."

Stevens and others assumed that freed blacks would most likely vote for the party that gave them their freedom—the Republican Party. They freely admitted that they hoped to strengthen their party in the South with black suffrage. Democrats in the South had led the call to form the Confederacy. Many Democrats in the North had opposed the Civil War. With the North's victory, the Republicans felt that they had a right to shape the governments and politics of the South.

In Their Own Words

Here is part of a speech that Thaddeus Stevens made to Congress in 1867, calling for black suffrage.

In the first place, it is just.... In the second place, it is a necessity in order to protect the loyal white men in the seceded States. The white Union men are in a great minority in each of those States. With them the blacks would act in a body...and the two united would form a majority, control the States, and protect themselves.

Johnson Leads the Attack on the Amendments

Almost as soon as he took office, President Andrew Johnson argued with Congress over Reconstruction. He, like many Southerners, strongly supported giving the states as much power as possible and limiting the power of the federal government. This "states' rights" view had been popular with slave owners, who had often argued that the federal government could not interfere with slavery and that each state had the right to decide on its own whether to allow slavery. With Reconstruction, Johnson believed that the federal government should focus on bringing the Southern states back into the Union. Instead, he believed, Congress was trying to use Reconstruction to change the role of government. The Republicans, he thought, were illegally trying to limit how the Southern states dealt with the freed slaves. Talking about the Fourteenth Amendment, he attacked the "concentration of all legislative powers in the national Government."

Johnson, like many Americans of the time, did not think that African Americans were ready to have the full legal rights of U.S. citizens. Some people argued that freedmen needed to be educated before they took part in public affairs. In his veto of the Civil Rights Act, Johnson said that it was unfair to grant immediate citizenship to freedmen who, because of slavery, were "less informed as to the nature and character of our institutions." Meanwhile, better-educated foreign immigrants had to prove that they were worthy of citizenship and the right to vote, which was not fair to these newcomers.

In general, Southern Democrats agreed with Johnson. The Southerners were also upset with the part of the Fourteenth Amendment that limited the political role of former Confederate leaders. That section was perhaps the main reason why the Southern states refused to ratify the amendment in 1866.

On the issue of black suffrage, some moderate Republicans joined Johnson in opposing the Radical Republicans. The moderates supported suffrage in the South, for the reasons that Stevens and others gave, but they were not ready to let free blacks in the North vote. In some states, free blacks had voted in the past, but by 1840, only about 7 percent of them had the right to vote. Some Northern Republicans feared that if they supported black suffrage, they would lose the votes of people who held racist views.

Elizabeth Cady Stanton and Susan B. Anthony had been demanding female suffrage for decades. They had also supported the abolition of slavery and civil rights for blacks. Because the Fifteenth Amendment did not include women, Stanton spoke out against it. She said that giving the vote to uneducated men—immigrants and freedmen—while denying that right to well-educated women was unfair.

Today, few Americans question the value of the Fifteenth Amendment or laws that protect voting rights. Lawyers and scholars, however, often debate the Fourteenth Amendment, which is cited in many legal

Fast Fact

The Fifteenth Amendment said that states could not take away voting rights based on a person's race. Some states, however, continued to limit who could vote by requiring citizens to prove that they could read or by making them pay a tax. These restrictions were aimed at poor African Americans.

cases. Some Americans still believe that it unfairly limits state powers. Yet that amendment has been used countless times to protect the civil rights of African Americans and other U.S. citizens facing discrimination.

THE 1866 CONGRESSIONAL ELECTIONS

U.S. presidential elections take place every four years. Every two years, however, voters choose members of the House and the Senate. One of the most famous "off-year" elections took place in 1866. The Fourteenth Amendment was at the heart of the campaign. In general, Republicans were for it, while President Johnson actively tried to elect politicians who opposed it and would support his Reconstruction plans. He made a tour of the country that was called "the swing around the circle." At one stop, he suggested that Thaddeus Stevens should be hanged. His comments on the tour helped Republicans win more seats in Congress. Starting in 1867, Republican lawmakers played an even bigger role in shaping Reconstruction.

In Their Own Words

Here is part of the statement that Andrew Johnson made in 1866 when he vetoed the Civil Rights Act. The ideas reflect how he felt about the Fourteenth Amendment, as well.

No such system as that contemplated by the details of this bill has ever before been proposed or adopted…. The distinction of race and color is by the bill made to operate in favor of the colored and against the white race. They interfere with [state laws], with the relations existing exclusively between the state and its citizens, or between inhabitants of the same state—an absorption and assumption of power by the general government [which would] break down the barriers which preserve the rights of the states.

CHAPTER TWELVE

The Impeachment of Andrew Johnson

WHAT

Congress accuses President Andrew Johnson of breaking the law.

ISSUES

The constitutionality of the Tenure of Office Act; Johnson's
policies after the Civil War

WHERE

Washington, D.C.

WHEN

1868

*A*s the end of the Civil War (1861–1865) neared, President Abraham Lincoln made plans for bringing the defeated South back into the Union. Lincoln, a Republican, wanted the process to be as peaceful as possible. However, he never had a chance to carry out his plans. On April 14, 1865, he was murdered while attending a play in Washington, D.C. Within hours, Vice President Andrew Johnson was sworn in as president. He would face the difficult job of leading the United States through the period known as Reconstruction. Johnson had to address the status of the newly freed slaves and create loyal governments in the defeated Southern states. To help him carry out Reconstruction policies, Johnson kept all the cabinet members who had served under President Lincoln.

At the start of the Civil War, Johnson had been a U.S. senator from Tennessee. A Democrat, he owned slaves, yet he opposed the political and economic interests of the South's rich and powerful slave owners. Johnson was also loyal to the Union. When Tennessee seceded, or left the Union, over slavery, Johnson stayed in Washington to help the Union cause. Lincoln rewarded that loyalty by naming Johnson the military governor of the parts of Tennessee that were captured by Union troops. Then, in 1864, the president asked him to run as his vice president.

Johnson was not well liked by Republican politicians. Politically, he supported states' rights—the idea that the federal government should not interfere with the state governments unless the Constitution specifically said that it could. Before the Civil War, Southern lawmakers had promoted the notion of states' rights to prevent the federal government from limiting slavery.

Fast Fact

The group of Southerners who assassinated Abraham Lincoln also plotted to kill other government leaders. Secretary of State William Seward was attacked in his home but survived. One assassin was supposed to kill Johnson, but the man lost his courage and didn't carry out the job.

During Reconstruction, Republicans in Congress believed that they had to take an active role in the Southern states. They wanted to guarantee the legal rights of African Americans and limit the power of the former leaders of the Confederate States of America. (The Confederacy was the government created by the eleven slaveholding states that had seceded from the Union.)

Johnson also held racist views that were common for the era. He thought that blacks did not have the same intelligence or skills as whites and that they should not have full political rights. That attitude conflicted with the beliefs of some Republicans, called the Radical Republicans, who wanted full legal equality between the races.

Many Republicans also disliked the new president personally. He was considered an uneducated, rural Democrat. He was stubborn and did not get along well with other politicians. However, Johnson was a successful politician known for his sharp speaking skills. He won support from many Southerners and from Northerners who opposed the Radicals.

Early Battles

At first, Radical Republicans welcomed Johnson's rise to the presidency. Johnson often said that the Confederates had committed treason by seceding from the Union, an idea that the Radicals shared. The crime of treason, an effort to overthrow or weaken a legal government, is the only one specifically mentioned in the U.S. Constitution.

Soon, however, the Radicals saw that Johnson did not share all their views on Reconstruction—particularly the need to help the newly freed slaves, called freedmen. Also, although Johnson said that treason should be punished, he wanted the Southern states to reenter the Union quickly. The federal government, he thought, should not slow down the process or place many restrictions on the Southern governments. The Radicals, however, believing that the

Southern states had sacrificed some of their rights by leaving the Union, did not want to be generous or forgiving.

In 1866, Congress passed the Civil Rights Act. This law was designed to make freedmen federal citizens so that they would have the same civil rights as whites. These included the right to own land, hold jobs, and have fair treatment in the courts. Johnson vetoed the act—he refused to sign it into law. In explaining his veto, he wrote that "the distinction of race and color is by the bill made to operate in favor of the colored and against the white race." Congress then used its constitutional power to pass the law despite the veto.

The Civil Rights Act was one of many that Congress passed despite Johnson's opposition. In March 1867 alone, Johnson vetoed three bills that Congress then voted into law without his approval. Two dealt with some of the details of Reconstruction. The third reflected the Radical Republicans' desire to limit Johnson's power as president. The Tenure of Office Act said that Johnson could not replace members of his cabinet without the Senate's approval. With this law, Republicans wanted to prevent Johnson from getting rid of government officials who supported their version of Reconstruction.

> *Fast Fact*
>
> A vetoed law can still go into effect if two-thirds of the members in both the U.S. House of Representatives and the U.S. Senate vote for it.

A MIDDLE COURSE

Within their party, the Radical Republicans represented just one view of Reconstruction. Other Republicans held more moderate views. They did not call for full equality between whites and blacks, and they were not as eager to punish former Confederates as the Radicals were. They also believed that Congress should work with Johnson as much as possible during Reconstruction. Over time, however, many moderates turned against Johnson. He did not consider their views, and he was unwilling to help the freedmen. The moderates began to support the Radicals' approach to Reconstruction.

The Stanton Affair and Impeachment

At the time that the Tenure of Office Act was passed, Johnson was feuding with Edwin Stanton, the secretary of war. The Tenure of Office Act meant that Johnson could not remove Stanton from his position. However, when Congress was not in session in August 1867, Johnson made plans to fire Stanton and replace him with General Ulysses S. Grant, one of the Union's greatest military heroes of the Civil War.

When Johnson asked Stanton to resign his post, the secretary refused. Johnson suspended him and named Grant to hold the job until Congress returned to Washington in the fall. Then Johnson would be required by law to explain why he had suspended Stanton, and Congress would decide whether or not to approve the decision. Johnson also replaced some of the Northern generals who were acting as military governors in the South.

In January, the Senate finally decided Stanton's fate. The lawmakers did not accept his suspension. Stanton then returned to his office and refused to leave. In February, the president ordered Stanton to step down and named General Lorenzo Thomas the new secretary of war.

For more than a year, the Radical Republicans had been searching for a reason to impeach Johnson. Impeachment is the first step in removing from office an elected official who has committed a crime. Under the Constitution, the House of Representatives first brings legal charges against the president. The Senate then decides if the president is guilty of those charges. If so, the president is removed from office. By firing Stanton in February without the Senate's approval, Johnson had violated the Tenure of Office Act. On February 24, 1868, the House of Representatives voted 128 to 47 that Johnson had committed several "high crimes and misdemeanors." His primary offense was disobeying the Tenure of Office Act.

Johnson's trial in the Senate began on March 13 and lasted more than two months. The Senate considered the eleven different alleged crimes, called articles of impeachment. On May 16, the Senate voted first on the last article of impeachment. This article was a summary of all the other articles, which dealt mostly with the Tenure of Office Act. The eleventh article also said that Johnson had earlier attacked Congress's legal right to pass laws. At that time, Congress had not included representatives from the Southern states, which Johnson thought was illegal.

Johnson's foes thought that this last article had the best chance of passing. They needed two-thirds of the senators, or thirty-six votes, to win. The Radicals ended up one vote short. The Senate then voted on two more articles. Each time, the result was the same: thirty-five to nineteen—one vote short of convicting Johnson. The president's opponents realized that they did not have enough votes to convict him on any of the charges. They decided to end the trial. Johnson had won, and he was convinced that he had done the right thing by challenging a law that he thought was unconstitutional. He served out the last few months of his term and left the White House in March 1869.

PRESIDENTIAL IMPEACHMENT

Besides Johnson, Bill Clinton is the only U.S. president to be impeached. The House of Representatives accused Clinton of lying during legal investigations of his personal affairs. The articles of impeachment also said that Clinton had tried to influence others to lie for him and that, by lying, he had abused his powers as president. In 1998, the Senate ruled that Clinton was not guilty.

In 1974, President Richard Nixon avoided impeachment by resigning from office. The proposed articles of impeachment dealt with Nixon's effort to hide his connection to a break-in at the Democratic Party's national headquarters. The scandal was known as Watergate, the name of the building where the break-in occurred.

Famous Figures

EDWIN STANTON
(1814–1869)

Born in Ohio, Edwin Stanton was trained as a lawyer. A Democrat, Stanton briefly served as U.S. attorney general under President James Buchanan. On slavery issues, however, he agreed with Republican policies. In 1862, Abraham Lincoln named Stanton his secretary of war, in which position Stanton improved the Union's system for purchasing military supplies. During the Tenure of Office crisis, Stanton lived for a time in his office, cooking his meals behind his locked door. Stanton finally left the government in May 1868. The next year, President Ulysses Grant named him to the U.S. Supreme Court, but Stanton died before he could fill the position.

The Case for Impeachment

The Radicals tried to use impeachment to get rid of Johnson and go forward with Reconstruction. They thought that the president had broken the law by trying to remove Stanton and by not carrying out a law that had been passed by Congress.

Presidents can veto laws that they think are unconstitutional, as Johnson had done with the Tenure of Office Act. However, Congress can override a veto, as it did with that law and several others. Johnson's duty as president was to make sure that all laws were carried out—even if he doubted their constitutionality. It was up to the courts, not him, to decide if the laws were unconstitutional.

During the impeachment trial, several members of the House of Representatives made the case against Johnson. George Boutwell of Massachusetts argued that the Tenure of Office Act was constitutional. The Constitution does not say specifically that the Senate has the power to stop the president from removing a cabinet member. Still, Boutwell argued that the Americans who drafted the Constitution wanted the Senate to play a role in filling government positions. This implied that the Senate should have a say in removing someone from office, as well as filling that office in the first place.

With their last two articles of impeachment, the House of Representatives went beyond the Tenure of Office Act. The lawmakers noted that on several occasions, Johnson had spoken out harshly against Radical Republicans. With those statements, the president "did attempt to bring into disgrace, ridicule, hatred, contempt and reproach, the Congress of the United States."

Outside of Congress, Republican newspapers and magazines also criticized the president's behavior. In September 1867, *Harper's Weekly* wrote that Johnson "could not be trusted. The law does not restrain him, for he denies the authority which makes it. The real situation at present is that the President asserts his will against the will of the people in Congress."

In Their Own Words

Charles Sumner of Massachusetts was one of the leading Radical Republicans in the Senate. Here is part of the statement that he made calling for Andrew Johnson's impeachment.

The veto power conferred by the Constitution as a remedy for ill-considered legislation was turned by [Johnson] into a weapon of offense against Congress and into an instrument to beat down...opposition.... The power of removal...was seized as an engine of tyranny and openly employed to maintain his wicked purposes by the sacrifice of good citizens who would not consent to be his tools.

A ticket to the impeachment trial of President Andrew Johnson from March 24, 1868.

Johnson Defends Himself

Even before the situation with Stanton, Johnson claimed that the Tenure of Office Act was unconstitutional. Under the Constitution, the Senate must approve new members of the cabinet. However, the Constitution does not say that the Senate plays any role in removing cabinet members once they have been approved. Johnson saw the new law as part of a pattern: Congress was trying to take away his powers, as outlined in the Constitution, so that it could control Reconstruction. In 1867, he wrote, "It is a great public wrong to take from the President powers conferred on him alone by the Constitution." To Johnson, the situation was not just about him personally. The office of the presidency and the American public were under attack.

Johnson claimed that he broke the Tenure of Office Act as part of a legal test. He wanted the Supreme Court to address the law and rule whether Congress had the power to pass it. To Johnson, the case was clear: The Constitution did not give Congress the power to stop a president from removing a cabinet member. Even if the law were constitutional, the president believed, it would not apply to Stanton. The wording of the Tenure of Office Act seemed to say that the law applied only to people actually appointed by the president. Lincoln, not Johnson, had made Stanton secretary of war.

At the trial in the Senate, Johnson's lawyers denied that the president had broken any laws. They also attacked the articles of impeachment that suggested that Johnson had weakened Congress's ability to carry out its duties. This charge was based on public comments that Johnson had made about Congress and the Radical Republicans who controlled it. The lawyers argued that Johnson had the same right to free speech as any other American.

Although Andrew Johnson found success as a politician, people did not tend to like him as a person. His presidency was marked by an almost constant battle between him and his opponents, resulting in his impeachment in 1868.

In Their Own Words

In the Senate, Republican James Grimes of Iowa voted to acquit, or find innocent, President Johnson. He cast the last vote on the first article of impeachment, guaranteeing that the president would not be found guilty. Here is part of the statement that Grimes made explaining his vote.

It is apparent to my mind that the President thoroughly believed the Tenure of Office Act to be unconstitutional and void. He was so advised by every member of his cabinet when the bill was presented to him for his approval in February 1867....

....The constitutional validity of this law could not be tested before the courts unless a case was made and presented to them. No such case could be made unless the President made a removal. That act of his would be necessarily the basis on which the case would rest.

Glossary

annul—to legally overturn a law or its effects

armory—a place where the government stores weapons

cabinet—a group of advisers to a leader

conspiracy—a plot among a group of people to carry out an illegal action

corruption—the use of illegal methods to gain money or power

despotism—a government system with one powerful ruler who denies citizens their freedom

discrimination—the unequal treatment of a person or group based on such traits as race, ethnic background, sex, or religion

dissenting—opposing the beliefs held by a majority

fugitive—a person who flees from legal authority, such as the police or a slave owner

inauguration—the ceremony giving an elected presidential candidate the powers of the office

latitude—imaginary lines circling the globe parallel to the equator that are used to indicate locations on Earth's surface

moral—correct, as defined by religious or legal teaching

naturalization—the process that makes an immigrant to a nation a legal citizen

petition—a request to the government to carry out some action, or the actual document making that request

plantations—large farms where usually just one crop is grown for sale

polls—places where citizens cast their votes

radical—extreme in thoughts or actions, compared to most members of a community

repeal—to overturn a law

resolution—a statement of belief or desire to take action

secede—to formally withdraw from a political organization

tyranny—a government system that denies individuals their freedom

Bibliography

BOOKS

Arnold, James R., and Roberta Wiener. *Divided in Two: The Road to Civil War, 1861.* Minneapolis: Lerner Publications, 2002.

Carey, Charles W., Jr. *The Mexican War: "Mr. Polk's War."* Berkeley Heights, NJ: Enslow Publishers, 2002.

Collier, Christopher, and James Lincoln Collier. *Slavery and the Coming of the Civil War, 1831–1861.* New York: Benchmark Books, 2000.

Fleischner, Jennifer. *The Dred Scott Case: Testing the Right to Live Free.* Brookfield, CT: Millbrook Press, 1997.

Hoig, Stan. *Night of the Cruel Moon: Cherokee Removal and the Trail of Tears.* New York: Facts on File, 1996.

Hughes, Christopher. *Andrew Johnson.* Woodbridge, CT: Blackbirch Press, 2001.

Johnston, Norma. *Remember the Ladies: The First Women's Rights Convention.* New York: Scholastic, 1995.

Roberts, Russell. *Lincoln and the Abolition of Slavery.* San Diego: Lucent Books, 2000.

Weber, Michael. *Civil War and Reconstruction.* Austin: Raintree Steck-Vaughn, 2001.

WEB SITES

African American Mosaic: Influence of Prominent Abolitionists
lcweb.loc.gov/exhibits/african/afam006.html

The Civil War
www.pbs.org/civilwar/

HarpWeek Presents...Finding Precedent: The Impeachment of Andrew Johnson
www.impeach-andrewjohnson.com/

National Humanities Center Online Professional Development Seminar Toolboxes— The Triumph of Nationalism/The House Dividing: Nationalism and Sectionalism in the United States: 1815–1850
www.nhc.rtp.nc.us/pds/triumphnationalism/triumphnationalism.htm

The U.S.-Mexican War (1846–1848) *www.pbs.org/kera/usmexicanwar/*

World Wide Web Virtual Library History Index—Reconstruction 1865–1880
www.ku.edu/history/VL/USA/ERAS/reconstruction.html

Cumulative Index

Confederate States of America,
    Vol. 3: 96–100, 102
confederation, Vol. 1: 133
Congregationalism, Vol. 1: 18, 60,
    61–68
Congregationalists. *See* Puritans
Congress. *See* U.S. Congress
conservative, Vol. 5: 133
conspiracy
    Vol. 3: 133
    Vol. 4: 133
Constitution, U.S.
    Vol. 1: 124–131, *127, 132*
    Vol. 2: 86
    Vol. 3: 92, 102
    Vol. 5: 131
Constitutional Convention, Vol.
    1: 107–108, 113–122, *118, 121*
Constitutional Equality
    Amendment (CEA), Vol. 5: 81
Constitutional Union Party,
    Vol. 3: 94
Continental Army, Vol. 1: 92
Continental Congress, Vol. 1:
    94–98, 102, 104–106
contras, Vol. 5: 89, 91, 94
Coolidge, Calvin, Vol. 4: 122
Cooper, Thomas, Vol. 2: 103
Corey, Giles, Vol. 1: 45
"corrupt bargain," Vol. 2: 109–112
corruption
    Vol. 1: 133
    Vol. 3: 133
    Vol. 4: 133
    Vol. 5: 133
Cosby, William, Vol. 1: 52–54, 55
Cotton, John, Vol. 1: 17–18, 19, *19*
Craig, Gregory, Vol. 5: *115*
Crawford, William, Vol. 2: 106
Creek, Vol. 3: 14
Crittenden, John, Vol. 3: 95, 100
Cuba, Vol. 4: 60–68, *61, 63*
Cunningham, Milton J., Vol. 4:
    57–58
Currie, Bettie, Vol. 5: 114
Czechoslovakia, Vol. 5: 26

D
Daughters of Liberty, Vol. 1: 73
Davenport, James, Vol. 1: 66, 68
Davis, Jefferson, Vol. 3: 96
Davis, John W., Vol. 5: 44–45
Dawes, William, Vol. 1: 83
Deane, Silas, Vol. 1: 104
The Death of Outrage (Bennett),
    Vol. 5: 119
death penalty, Vol. 1: 42
debatable issues
    Vol. 1: 7–9
    Vol. 2: 7–9
    Vol. 3: 7–9
    Vol. 4: 7–9
    Vol. 5: 7–9
Declaration of Independence
    Vol. 1:
        Abigail Adams, *100*
        arguments against inde-
            pendence, 99–102
        debate for independence,
            95–99

precursors to, 92–94
    writing of, 94–95, 96
"Declaration of the Causes and
    Necessity of Taking Up Arms"
    (Dickinson and Jefferson),
    Vol. 1: 92
"Declaration in the Name of the
    People" (Bacon), Vol. 1: 38
"Declaration of Rights and
    Sentiments" (Stanton)
    Vol. 3: 58
    Vol. 4: 110
Declaratory Act, Vol. 1: 77–78
DeJarnette, Daniel, Vol. 3: 98
Delancey, James, Vol. 1: 53, 54,
    55–56
Delancey, Stephen, Vol. 1: 52
de Lôme, Enrique Dupuy,
    Vol. 4: 62
Democratic Party
    Vol. 3:
        civil rights for African
            Americans and, 117,
            119
        Compromise of 1850 and,
            67, 69
        emancipation and, 106
        slavery and, 93
        Texas annexation and,
            36–38
        Thirteenth Amendment
            and, 109
    Vol. 4:
        Chinese and, 36
        election of 1876 and,
            12–20
        League of Nations and,
            93–94
        Prohibition and, 104
    Vol. 5: 116, 117, 122–132
Democratic-Republican Party
    Vol. 2:
        Alien and Sedition Acts
            and, 25–28
        defense of Embargo Acts,
            69–70
        elections issues of 1800,
            38–40
        Jay's Treaty and, 15–16,
            17, 20
        overview of, 12
        War of 1812 and,
            81–82, 84
        XYZ affair and, 23
depression, Vol. 3: 22
despotism
    Vol. 1: 133
    Vol. 3: 133
    Vol. 4: 133
Detroit Free Press, Vol. 3: 78
Dewey, George, Vol. 4: 63
DeWitt, John, Vol. 5: 19, 21
Dickens, Charles, Vol. 2: 104
Dickinson, John, Vol. 1: 92, 93,
    102, 105
Diem, Ngo Dinh,
    Vol. 5: 49, 50, 51
discrimination
    Vol. 3: 133
    Vol. 4: 133
    Vol. 5: 133.

See also racism; reverse
    discrimination
dissenting
    Vol. 3: 133
    Vol. 4: 133
    Vol. 5: 133
disunion, Vol. 3: 64
Doe v. Bolton, Vol. 5: 67
Donelson, Andrew Jackson,
    Vol. 2: 111
Douglass, Frederick, Vol. 3: 54,
    103
Douglas, Stephen
    Vol. 3:
        in election of 1860, 93,
            94, 94
        Kansas-Nebraska Act
            of, 73
        Nebraska Territory
            and, 77
        portrait of, 79
        secession of Southern
            states and, 100
Douglas, William O., Vol. 5: 34
draft, Vol. 5: 58, 59
Dred Scott case, Vol. 3:
    82–90, 83
Duane, William, Vol. 3: 25
Du Bois, W.E.B., Vol. 5: 45
due process, Vol. 4: 56, 57–58
Durbin, Richard, Vol. 5: 120
Dutch Reformed Church, Vol. 1:
    60, 64

E
Easton, John, Vol. 1: 29
economy (1930s),
    Vol. 4: 122–132
education
    Vol. 5:
        affirmative action,
            100–110, *101, 103,
            104, 107*
        *Brown v. Board of
            Education*, 36–46,
            38, 44
Edwards, Jonathan,
    Vol. 1: 62, *62*, 63, 65
Eighteenth Amendment, Vol. 4:
    102–103, *106, 107*
Eisenhower, Dwight, Vol. 5: 46,
    49, 56
election of 1800, Vol. 2: 32–40
election of 1824,
    Vol. 2: 106–112, *107*
election of 1876, Vol. 4: 12–20,
    13, 16, 18
election of 2000. *See* presidential
    election of 2000
Electoral College
    Vol. 2: 35
    Vol. 5: *123*
Electoral Commission,
    Vol. 4: *16,* 16–20
electoral vote
    Vol. 4: 14–20
    Vol. 5: 123
electors, Vol. 2: 34, 35
Elliot, Roderick, Vol. 5: 38
Ellsberg, Daniel, Vol. 5: 60
El Salvador, Vol. 5: 88–89, 90